Karen Green

How to Make a Perfect Smoothie

A Step by Step Guide
to the Art, Features,
and Science of Smoothies

The Smoothie Recipe Book

D1293738

Content

Content..3

Introduction 7

What is a Smoothie? 9

Smoothies - a Story of Bright Taste 13

Smoothies - Food or Drink? 16

Types and Categories of Smoothies..22

Why are Smoothies beneficial? 27

   15 Reasons to Drink Smoothies Daily 28

Disadvantages and Contraindications of Smoothies that You Need to Know About...34

Rules for Consuming Smoothies 37

The Perfect Smoothie Formula 39

   Liquid Base for Smoothies...40

   Base Ingredients 41

   Natural Additives 44

   Need Fats for a Smoothie? 44

   What is the Correct Ratio of Ingredients for a Smoothie? 45

List of Products that Cannot Be Mixed..48

How to Make a Smoothie: 7 Easy Steps 50

Key Rules for Making a Real Healthy Smoothie 54

Color Rules for Smoothies 58

Common Smoothies Errors and Ways around Them 61

How to Choose an Ideal Blender for Smoothies 65

   Types of blenders 66

What should you look for when buying a blender?..66

FAQ about Smoothies **68**

Healthy Quick & Easy Smoothies Recipe Book.....................................**71**

Smoothies for Breakfast **72**

Smoothie Tropical Breakfast..72

Berry & Pomegranate Smoothie 74

Banana & Sweet Cherry Smoothie 75

Smoothie with Pineapple, Dates, and Peanuts 76

Smoothie Poppy Surprise 78

Banana, Avocado, and Hempseed Smoothie 80

Strawberry Yoghurt Smoothie with Pistachios..81

Dried Fruit & Walnut Smoothie 82

Smoothie with Persimmon, Pumpkin, and Nuts 84

Tofu Banana Vanilla Smoothie 86

Savory Strawberries Blueberries Smoothie 87

Pear & Walnut Smoothie 88

Hearty Fruit Chia Smoothie 90

Vegetable Smoothies for Lunch and Dinner.......................................**92**

Savory Cauliflower-Garlic Smoothie 92

Zucchini & Greens Smoothie 93

Carrot & Celery Smoothie 94

Broccoli, Apple & Lime 95

Broccoli & Lettuce Smoothie 96

Carrots & Spice Smoothie 97

Pumpkin Smoothie with Apples 98

Pumpkin Citrus Smoothie with Ginger 100

Pumpkin Pie 101

Mint Cucumber 102

Green Health 103

Thick Tomato & Bell Pepper 104

4

Sweet Pepper, Cucumber, & Ginger...106

Carrot Smoothie for a Great Mood 107

Smoothie with Beetroot, Carrot, and Apple 108

Cucumber Freshness...109

Savory Zucchini with Herbs and Garlic 110

Beetroot & Strawberry Smoothie 111

Green Smoothies for Health **112**

Powerful Slimming Smoothie...112

Spicy Spinach 114

Pineapple-Ginger Smoothie with Spinach 115

Super Vitamin Bomb Smoothie 116

Spinach with Avocado and Grapes 117

Arugula & Avocado Detox Smoothie 118

Spinach & Apples Smoothies 120

Avocado & Spinach 121

Ginger Mint Smoothie..122

Avocado, Kiwi & Parsley 124

Super Vitamin Celery Smoothie 125

Celery & Oatmeal...126

Fruit & Berry Smoothies..**127**

Berry Vanilla Smoothie...127

Strawberries, Raspberries & Kiwi 128

Tropical Fruit Spinach Smoothie 129

Raspberry Surprise...130

Vanilla Mango Smoothie 131

Pineapple Perfection 132

Spicy Ginger-Pear Surprise 133

Lemon Banana Smoothie 134

Peach Surprise 136

Banana Strawberry Chia Smoothie 137

Spicy Cherry Smoothie...138

Cherries & Banana 139

Blueberry Pineapple Smoothie 140

Summer Apple Banana Smoothie 141

Apple & Pineapple 142

Cream Peaches...143

Spicy Ginger-Strawberry Smoothie 144

Iced Apple & Spice Smoothie 145

Gooseberry & Blackberry Mint Smoothie...146

Wonderful Watermelon Smoothie..148

Crazy Savory Cranberries Smoothie 149

Smoothie Desserts **150**

Strawberry with Ice Cream and Pistachios 150

Smoothie Tropical Paradise...151

Chocolate Cherry Smoothie..152

Strawberry Banana Smoothie Dessert 154

Banana-Pistachio Smoothie with Cocoa 156

Banana, Kiwi, and Creamy Ice Cream Smoothie.................................158

Banana Almond Chocolate Smoothie 160

Apricot-Coffee & Chocolate Smoothie 162

Chocolate Black Bean Smoothie...164

Conclusion **165**

Introduction

The sound of a blender mixing smoothies has been heard regularly in our kitchen for five years now. Over the years, smoothies have become as familiar a snack to me as scrambled eggs, oatmeal, or a sandwich to someone else. And what could be healthier and more natural than making a fresh fruit or vegetable puree and mixing it with water or milk?

Why are both adults and children so fond of smoothies? Because this gentle, soft, refreshing drink is truly delicious! Smoothies are loved by everyone who has tried this drink at least once in their life. Who wouldn't like shredded fruit? The dense structure of the smoothie allows you to drink it slowly, besides, smoothies always turn out bright and colorful, they please the eye. Children like it for its taste and color, and adults like that, having tasted a delicate dessert in a restaurant, they feel lightness ...

A smoothie is one of the loveliest, simplest, and most enjoyable drinks that most people still underestimate. It is among the tastiest and most popular drinks in the world. Take a ride to the largest Indian cities, visit the most popular Mediterranean communities, and tour most of the North American Districts. There is hardly a restaurant in these urban communities without a smoothie on their menu.

Smoothies are so popular that they are often served at official gatherings, business meetings, and occasions beyond the evening booze and general restaurants. Smoothies have burst into our lives as fast as Asian dishes, chia seeds, and goji berries. They are drunk by Hollywood stars advised by famous nutritionists and recommended by fans of healthy eating and nutritionists.

But despite the popularity of smoothies around the world, many have questions and doubts about smoothies.

➤ Smoothies are good. Or not?
➤ Or not all smoothies, but only vegetable ones? What's the best way to make them?
➤ And what to put into smoothies and what if the stomach swells from them?
➤ But what about the rule that vegetables should only be eaten separately from fruit?
➤ Is smoothie a healthy treat or a high-calorie dessert?
➤ Are there any special "correct" proportions or other rules for making smoothies? ...

Familiar questions? I get asked these all the time.

So... Haven't made a smoothie before, want to start making one, and need more information?

Or are smoothies already part of your menu and you want to know more about them?

If you are looking for answers to these and other smoothie questions, and also want to know how to drink a smoothie properly or when to drink a smoothie, then you are in the right place.

Right now, you are about to open a book that captures the concept of smoothies swiftly. It shows you a comprehensive picture of smoothies, their benefits, recipes, and procedures, among other things. You will learn the easiest, liveliest, and quickest ways to make nutritious smoothies.

If you know nothing at all, the next few pages will take you from a complete beginner to a master who understands the art and value of smoothies. Equally, you will add a lot of information and recipes to the ones you have always known.

Importantly, you must be open to new information. You must be prepared to learn new arts, correct inappropriate ones, and be willing to practice the new styles you are about to acquire. When all of these are on standby, I strongly suggest you flip the page and head right on to the main content in the book.

I will tell you not just about smoothies, but about the RIGHT smoothies, that will not only energize you but will also become your basis for proper nutrition for years to come. Following my simple recommendations, you can come up with your own original recipes without the fear of spoiling anything - you will always get a deliciously tasty and healthy smoothie!

Find a complete guide to making smoothies here and learn how to make stunning, delicious, and truly healthy drinks. So...

To the smoothie enthusiasts,

Cheers!

What is a Smoothie?

The name smoothie comes from the English word "smooth", which means soft, smooth, tender. Indeed, all three terms are great for smoothies. This is exactly what a smoothie feels like - a fruit or vegetable texture mass whipped in a blender, thick enough not to be a cocktail, something between juice and puree. It is a thick drink that is eaten rather than drunk.

A smoothie is a thick drink, whipped to a homogeneous mass that is made from raw fruits, nuts, spices, herbal supplements, liquids, and vegetables. It is a creative mix of natural fruit, legumes, and veg with a little touch of spices. Ice, juice, milk, yogurt, nuts, honey, and even eggs are added to it. By and large, any kind of food can be in a smoothie. For example, green teas, herbs, honey, oatmeal - in general, anything that is loved or considered acceptable to the consumer.

Smoothies are fruit, vegetable, berry, fruit and berry, fruit and vegetable, red or green, dairy or vegan, even based on algae. In addition, they include refreshing (sugar-free), saturating (very thick), dessert (sweet), cold (with a high ice content).

Smoothie is usually blended in a way that it sometimes forms a creamy paste or liquid. Regardless of what you form, a smoothie is always tasty and easy to make. You may have it as a quick breakfast. You may equally have it as dinner or something in-between snacks and brunch.

In most cases, a smoothie isn't a blend of only one or two items. You would have to mix a little bit of everything to get nice flavors. You can even go as far as five to six components, and you will always get a flavor that fills your nose and lungs with a delight you cannot find words to describe.

One of the brightest things about taking a smoothie is that you are hardly limited by your food preferences. You can make several smoothies as a vegan. You can have them as a vegetarian or an omnivore too. The only difference is that you are open to fewer recipes as a vegan or a vegetarian.

You can equally have smoothies as an athlete, a pregnant person, a child, or an adult unless you have strict health complications that require you to steer clear of smoothies and their ingredients.

We are talking about one of the fastest and relatively comfortable diets that are available for everyone in this book. Smoothies are easy meals that you can make on a tight schedule. They are smart and entertaining choices for your friends who are coming over too. You only have to be creative about it, and you can stuff your friends with a different blend, flavor, and mix of smoothies every time they stop over.

To get you started, here are a few things that will make you love smoothies:

Smoothies are a dish for every taste and budget

What is growing in the beds now? What's in the refrigerator? Into the blender! Buzz - buzz, pour into a tall glass, wine glass, bowl, decorate with a berry, a piece of fruit, sprinkle with nuts, chocolate, coconut chips - mmm! How delicious it is! And be sure to eat smoothies by sipping them through a thick tube or with a spoon.

Smoothies are a universal drink

Imagine a remarkably refreshing drink that quenches both thirst and hunger, can relieve heartburn, improves digestion, removes toxins, promotes fat burning and recovery after exercise, saturates the body with vitamins and energy, strengthens immunity, reduces cravings for sweets and it is also very, very tasty.

Smoothies are ready to satisfy any desire - in taste, color, calories, and consistency

Some smoothie bars even have special consultants who help the visitor to choose with the help of leading questions: "Which smoothie should you serve? To relax? Collect your thoughts? Cheer up? "

Smoothies are simple, beautiful, and very healthy

Just one glass of smoothie "fits" a full breakfast or dinner, a lot of necessary microelements, and a good mood. Smoothie has become synonymous with healthy eating and beauty. Many people believe that it contributes to weight loss and increased vitality. Drinking a delicious thick shake, we get a portion of protein for building cells, carbohydrates for vitality, and antioxidants and trace elements to fill deficiencies.

Smoothies are a quick, delicious, and easy way to add nutrients to your diet, as well as your child's.

Smoothies are one of the healthiest eating options and synonymous with a great snack

A properly prepared smoothie is a great option for a cleansing breakfast, a healthy dinner, or a fasting day. It can be prepared in advance and stored in the refrigerator! Or you can pour it into a bottle and take it with you to work or training! It is convenient to give children to school with them so that they can saturate their bodies with vitamins during breaks! Smoothies help to boost immunity and improve well-being through vitamins, as well as cheer us up with their vibrant color.

Smoothies are a very tasty thick drink, a dish, a dessert, a cocktail, and a sorbet - for every taste!

It all depends on what you put in the container for the mixture - the flight of imagination is not limited here. Depending on the recipe from which it is prepared, it is suitable for both weight loss and weight gain. It can be drunk in the morning instead of breakfast, it can be consumed by adding protein before exercise, it can be part of sports nutrition. Smoothies are also a healthy alternative to traditional desserts.

Smoothies have an endless variety of flavors that you can constantly experiment with

The technology for making smoothies is incredibly simple. All that is needed is just a few free minutes, the right fresh food, a working blender, a little imagination and inspiration, and a huge desire to create another culinary masterpiece.

Simple recipes are within the power of not only experienced housewives, but even those who are generally far from cuisine and cooking. And the ability to combine smoothie components in a variety of combinations will appeal to both lazy chefs and lovers of experimentation.

Smoothies – who are they suitable for?

For active, for healthy, for positive people, for adults, for children, for the elderly, for athletes, for fitness lovers, for women, for men, for larks and owls, for vegetarians, for strict vegans / raw foodists, for diabetics, for lovers of sweets, for large, for thin, for those who follow a diet ... - the list goes on. But one thing is clear: smoothies are for everyone!

Today, smoothies have also become the basis of a new direction in the field of healthy eating. Millions of followers of smoothie diets consider these shakes to be an excellent way to lose weight and maintain vitality.

Put your business aside, make a smoothie right now and sing its funny name: S-M-O-O-T-H-I-E ... Music of delight! Fireworks of taste! Allow yourself at least occasionally to be a child, enjoying a healthy dessert.

Smoothies - a Story of Bright Taste

Each of us has heard the word "smoothie" at least once in our life, moreover, many have tried this outlandish delicacy more than once. However, few people know where this non-standard drink that can replace ordinary food came from.

The method of converting products into mashed potatoes existed even in ancient times, and among all the peoples of the world. For centuries, people of Mediterranean and Eastern culture have made drinks from fresh fruits that resembled what we call smoothies today. For example, the ancient Indians drank guava juice with pulp before hunting or fighting to strengthen their spirit and gain stamina. Refreshing drinks based on crushed fruits and berries are widespread in hot tropical countries. It is believed that how to make smoothies was invented in Latin America. It is from there that the tradition of serving freshly squeezed juices and chopped fruits with ice originates. The mention of drinks similar to smoothies is found in other nations as well. Before a battle, the Polish gentry drank a drink made from beer, a few eggs, and thick sour cream. And what about Slavic oat jelly, which is described in ancient chronicles? Or an Indian rice drink and all kinds of French puree soups? Don't they look like smoothies?

According to another version, the fashion for healthy eating in the form of smoothies came from Pacific surfers, who found it much easier to drink food than chew when a huge wave was moving towards them.

California is considered to be the birthplace of smoothies. Flamboyant bottles of fruit and berry drinks with pulp and ice began selling in California health food stores in the 1930s.

The first wave of popularity of smoothies came with the massive appearance of refrigerators and freezers in homes. After people discovered the ability to freeze fruit and fresh milk right in their kitchens, Stephen Poplavsky invented another popular kitchen appliance, the blender, which was originally used as a mixer. It is interesting and curious how the invention of one thing can cause the invention of something completely different. Chefs have long since cut and rubbed the ingredients of dishes with their own hands, but Poplavsky's blender was the first appliance with a rotating blade at the bottom of the container. This made it very convenient for them to make milkshakes.

In 1935 Fred Osius improved on Poplavsky's invention and created the famous Waring Blender. It was with this homemade technique that making smoothies became a matter of minutes. When Osius told reporters that his blender would revolutionize American drinks, he had no idea how true his prediction would be!

Later, the Vita-Mix blender appeared, which revolutionized its environment, because it was able to grind raw vegetables and nuts into a smooth paste.

With the invention and use of both blenders and refrigerators, smoothies began to gain popularity during the 30s, 40s, and 50s. The first glory of smoothies was recognized in the 1960s when vegetarianism began to gain more and more popularity, and the wave of smoothies swept across various countries. Then the recipes included fruit, juices and ice, and less often - frozen milk. These cocktails were offered in restaurants and health food stores along with tofu, fruits, carob, and other diet foods.

It is also said that the fashion for smoothies was introduced in the 1960s by the "flower children" traveling around the world - hippies. They argued that the grated fruit with juice is the "food of the sun" and therefore the smoothie has become a favorite drink of non-standard youth. As a result, the smoothie has gained genuine popularity and universal acceptance, becoming one of the most beloved drinks in most of the world.

But real fame came to smoothies only in the late 60s. The world began to go crazy with this simple and amazingly delicious find. During this time, a massive fascination with healthy food, fitness, and macrobiotic nutrition began in the United States. Smoothies gained incredible popularity among those who want to look good and be healthy. Smoothies began to be produced on an industrial scale. Health food stores began to appear in great numbers in all states of the country, and these stores began to sell thick drinks made from crushed fruits. Fans of a balanced diet immediately appreciated the fresh fruit and vegetable shake as a source of the right calories and vitamins.

A young and insanely popular bodybuilder named Arnold Schwarzenegger drank a pitcher of smoothie after his intense workouts. Another famous bodybuilder of the time, and twice Schwarzenegger's age, Lalane was also one of the zealous supporters of smoothies and healthy eating - there was even a whole TV show where he advertised the benefits of healthy eating and juicing smoothies, he was also the first person in the United

States to sell food TV supplements. Lalaine opened the first health and fitness club to promote healthy eating and, in particular, smoothie juices (some of his recipes are some of the most popular on the Internet today).

Food companies seized on the trend and began promoting smoothies in the food market. According to Dan Tit, director of the Smoothie Association, health food stores began selling fruit juices and fresh fruit drinks to meet the demand and interest of an increasing number of macrobiotic diets and health-conscious people. In addition, by this time, many families had the opportunity to buy fresh fruit from exotic countries throughout the year. Freezers appeared, which meant that people could buy cheap seasonal fruits and freeze them for future use. The popularity of smoothies grew before our eyes.

The name "smoothie" itself went down in history with the light hand of the founder of the "Smoothie King" chain of cocktail bars, Stephen Kuhnau, who in those years came up with it. In 1973, Stephen Kahnau founded the first smoothie bar, Smoothie King in Louisiana, and began selling mixed fruit cocktails called smoothies. He experimented with smoothie recipes for years, adding yogurt, protein powder, and vitamins to them. Over the next three decades, Smoothie King bars will spread across the country and made the term smoothie a common word.

In the 80s, a lot of attention was paid to sports, and a healthy lifestyle was incredibly fashionable, so smoothies became an integral part of many people. At that time, specialized fresh bars began to open in the United States, where the main dish on the menu was smoothies enriched with useful minerals and multivitamins.

The peak in popularity of smoothies is directly related to the 1984 Los Angeles Olympics, for which these original and healthy drinks were developed especially. It was logical to offer not hamburgers as a snack, but these tasty and healthy drinks.

The healthy cocktail gained real worldwide popularity in the 1990s - in part because bottles of this drink began to be sold in regular stores and supermarkets. Then the green smoothie was invented. By the 2000s, the production and sale of smoothies in the United States had become an entire industry.

Over the years, smoothies have come a long way and are popular not only in America but around the world. And with the advent of the trend towards a healthy lifestyle, which only continues to grow, a delicious cocktail is becoming a familiar "dish" on the regular home menu.

Smoothies - Food or Drink?

Up to today, there is an active debate about what a smoothie is - food or drink?

Some confidently call it a cocktail, considering it a drink, but nutritionists assure us: smoothies are food! And this has its own logic: the thick whipped consistency of solid food is a simple and amazingly appetizing find that can replace a full meal.

Simply put, smoothies are food you can drink.

A smoothie is a drink and food at the same time!

One way or another, hardly anyone will argue with the fact that the most important thing in a smoothie is its extremely attractive taste and useful properties.

How is a smoothie different from a cocktail?

As hinted earlier, a smoothie is a drink that is made of fruit and veggies. You may have a blend of several fruits and syrups, but the central ingredients are always derived from veggies and fruits. Apart from these, protein and ice may be added to strike a balance. Due to the natural composition of smoothies, they are usually tasty, and relatively safe for your health. They smell nice, and they are easy to make too. You can hardly have a health complication that would require you to stop eating fruit. It is also impossible to be too young or old for veggies too. This is why a smoothie has no age barrier, and it often contributes to health.

On a similar outlook, a cocktail is a blend of different ingredients including fruits. It is only different from a smoothie in that it requires a lot more. Typically, alcohol, fruit juice, and syrup are added to a cocktail. Most cocktail recipes also contain ice cream and a lot of sugar in the form of honey, chocolate syrup, and other sweet additives. But the classic smoothie is traditionally made without dairy products and sugar and includes only natural, unprocessed ingredients.

This implies that a cocktail goes beyond natural fruit and syrups to include alcoholic drinks. By implication, it becomes impossible for children, pregnant women, and people with certain health complications to have a cocktail. Apart from that, the taste is always different from that of a casual smoothie and you can get intoxicated on a cocktail. While a smoothie is healthier, safer, and tastier than a cocktail, a cocktail may be preferred at night parties and adult parties. Common cocktails are Mojito, Pinacolada, Tequilla Sunrise, Margaritas, and others.

I must tell you; smoothies are not the non-alcoholic version of cocktails. If you are wondering what that would be, then 'mocktail' is the answer. Mocktails are made like smoothies. The distinguishing punch is that they have got soft drinks and nonalcoholic syrups in place of the alcohol in cocktails. Mocktails include ice and fruit juices too. You'd hardly find unprocessed fruit here. So, there you have it. A smoothie is not a cocktail, and it is not a mocktail.

How is a smoothie different from a lassi?

Smoothies are not considerably different from lassi. This is the main reason most people often confuse them. They usually contain similar ingredients, and they are almost substitutes for each other. Despite that, there is a landmark distinction that cannot be written off.

Lassi is a traditional yogurt-based drink originating from the Indian subcontinent.

Traditional lassi is a salty drink made from yogurt and water and spiced. Nowadays, sweet, fruity lassis, which are made from natural yogurt, spices (usually cardamom), and pureed fruit, are gaining special popularity outside the homeland of the drink.

So what's the difference between a lassi and a smoothie, as both are whipped fruit drinks?

First of all, the difference from smoothies is the taste and composition of lassi:

> ➢ yogurt

- ➢ water (not always, but often)
- ➢ cardamom
- ➢ one (!) Puréed fruit such as mango, strawberry, or banana.

In a Nepalese restaurant, I was told that they add canned mango to the mango lassi, which is easy to whip and already contains sugar, so they don't add any additional sweetener to the recipe.

So, while each of these may contain elements of the other, they are relatively different, and their priorities are not the same. One last thing, a smoothie is always healthier than a lassi.

How is a smoothie different from a milkshake?

Milkshakes and smoothies are not particularly different from each other. Just like lassi and smoothies, the recipes used for milkshakes and smoothies are not particularly different. The basic difference lies in their recipes and their nutritional information.

On average, a smoothie would tilt towards fruits, flavors, and similar syrups. On the flip side, milkshakes include more dairy products like milk, fruits, and syrups. If you are a kid or chocolate fan reading this, you will be excited to know that you can have more chocolate syrups, candy syrups, and so forth in milkshakes. That might make it unhealthier when compared with a smoothie.

How is a smoothie different from a freshly squeezed juice?

Let's begin with the slightest difference. You make smoothies with whipped whole fruits and vegetables by blending the ingredients. You are likely going to squash the ingredients in a blender till it all forms something pasty or liquid and in the end, you get a thick and quite satisfying drink that contains pulp and looks more like a liquid fruit puree. This means that you get all the fruit and fiber in your drink.

On the flip side, freshly squeezed juice is not like that.

A freshly squeezed juice is extracted from the same source as a smoothie i.e. fruit, vegetables, greens, and so on. But the production process and final results are comparatively not the same. Typically, you do not squash your ingredients when making freshly squeezed juice. You extract them. You use the fruit in a way that only the juice or the liquid is collected from them. Every other item, particularly the fiber will be missed out.

This means one thing, a freshly squeezed juice will miss out on the nutrients in the fruit or legume that are not contained in the juice, while a smoothie captures it all. Fiber is an integral part of the diet that helps to stabilize the digestion process. With it, your body system is provided enough water and flexibility to digest pretty much everything.

Fiber should be taken moderately to avoid stomach disorders. Moderately or not, you can't have it in a freshly squeezed juice, and a smoothie doesn't leave it out. That's one big difference between a smoothie and a freshly squeezed juice.

In addition, freshly squeezed juices are often criticized by nutritionists for their high sugar concentration, which leads to a sharp rise in blood sugar levels.

But thanks to the long-digesting fiber, which is in the smoothie, sugar is absorbed much more slowly and does not cause severe drops in blood sugar, which are usually followed by the feeling of the year and, as a result, excessive consumption of calories. This undoubtedly makes smoothies a healthier drink.

Moreover, despite the usefulness of freshly squeezed juice, it cannot provide the body with all the substances necessary for health by itself. Unlike smoothies, juice is unlikely to be able to fully replace food intake and satisfy hunger.

On the other hand, a smoothie can become your complex breakfast, lunch, or dinner. Unlike freshly squeezed juices, which invigorate instantly, but for a short time, like a vitamin "explosion", smoothies give a long-lasting feeling of satiety due to the presence of pulp and a combination of different tastes.

Smoothie or juice - which is healthier?

Fresh or not, a juice remains the same. If you have read this chapter from the start, you've probably figured that juice is extracted from its ingredients while the same ingredients must be crushed before a smoothie is made. When juice is fresh, you do not have to add flavors or syrups. When it is no longer fresh, however, you may have to consider stimulants, additives, and complementary sugar. In most cases, ice and fruit syrups are the supplementary ingredients required for a great smoothie.

If you follow that up, some facts will become automatically apparent to you. First, smoothies are as natural as they can be. They contain healthy options that the body requires for the efficiency of several internal systems; the digestive system especially. If consistently taken, smoothies can help you cover some deficiencies in your food intake and body nutrients.

On the other side of the fence, juice may not contain as many nutrients. We have earlier pointed out that fiber is missed out when fruit and legumes are squeezed, and not squashed. This means no matter the amount you eat, you'll have to supplement fiber. It gives the clue that juices are one-stop short of smoothies.

Besides this, juice can sometimes be supplemented with additives and condiments. Preservatives may equally be used when the juice has to be preserved. When all of these are considered up, you realize that a smoothie is unquestionably healthier than juice.

Now, we have set smoothie apart from every other drink or diet that might look like it. We have identified their differences and it is time we focused on a smoothie in its entirety. We know what it is already, but what are its uses, and why is it a smart choice for anyone?

Types and Categories of Smoothies

Let's delve deeper. You can already distinguish a smoothie from everything else. You know exactly why a smoothie isn't like anything else, and you know the general rule that applies to the consumption of smoothies.

Let's dive deeper into the different categories of smoothies and their respective importance.

Nutritionist Ansley Hill once reported that smoothies can supply nutrients that reduce inflammation, improve digestion, and lower your risk of chronic conditions like heart disease and obesity. You have also discovered several beneficial advantages of smoothies in the previous pages. To be specific, smoothies can be prepared to improve health. They can be prepared to ensure that you consume the necessary nutrients. They are particularly helpful for athletes, children, and pregnant women who may have no appetite to consume a healthy diet while trying to meet their daily calorie needs. Smoothies like these usually contain fruit, veg, and any ingredients that each person is deficient in.

Green or Vegetable Smoothies

Green or Vegetable smoothies are smoothies primarily made with green veggies. We are talking about smoothies that contain spinach, leafy veggies in general, Swiss Chard, and dark leafy greens.

Green smoothies are the healthiest ones, as they contain a large amount of greens (20-40% of the total) and unsweetened fruits and even vegetables (for example, cucumber). They are easily absorbed by the body and are a great way to increase your greens intake in your regular diet. Greens also have a huge list of useful properties (alkalizing, fighting inflammation, delivering oxygen to cells, and they contain a huge amount of vitamins and minerals). There are a lot of benefits attributed to eating green smoothies, particularly when your veggie intake is nothing to be proud of.

A 2018 study indicates that less than 10% of Americans meet their daily veggie needs. So, if you recognize that you are becoming deficient in veggies and you need a convenient way to get them in, green smoothies should be your best pick.

Fruit and Berry Smoothies

Fruit and berry smoothies are the most popular, as most smoothies are made with fruit. They usually taste rather sweet and pleasant. When making random smoothie recipes, the first thing you'll probably think about is fruit. Berry smoothies are real antioxidant "bombs" for the body thanks to the addition of berries (strawberries, raspberries, blueberries, currants, cherries, etc.).

Detox or Slimming Smoothies

A detox smoothie includes ingredients that can facilitate detoxification in your body. Typically, detox smoothies are made from green vegetables and fruit, which have a healing effect on our bodies. Almost all of them are low in calories, but very rich in vitamins and minerals. In addition, green vegetables and fruit are great for cleansing our bodies. They improve metabolism. These are usually smoothies that contain minimal sugar and are made with water instead of yogurt, milk, or cottage cheese. They also often contain healthy fats such as flaxseed or almond oil, which can help make the drink richer.

Caffeine stimulants such as green tea or coffee can also be added to weight loss smoothies as they promote weight loss by boosting metabolism and decreasing appetite. Do it or not, your body system will find a way to detoxify. You can only fast-track things by trying out a detox smoothie or a detoxification technique. It must be stressed that a detox smoothie cannot completely detox your body. It can only facilitate the process.

Dessert Smoothies

In addition to smoothies prepared as a main course, smoothies can also be prepared as a dessert. Dessert smoothies are a healthy alternative to traditional milkshakes and are often made with nut milk, superfoods, dried fruit, and spices, but they can sometimes contain more sugar and less wholesome ingredients like ice cream, chocolate, cookies, marshmallows, etc. A dessert smoothie is any that you prepare solely to sip after a proper meal. You are not using it as the main course this time, you are having it to "wash down" what you have eaten.

Baby Smoothies

Baby smoothies are primarily intended for babies and children who are no longer breastfeeding. All parents want their children to grow up healthy but getting children to eat healthy food is not always easy. And if many children love sweet fruits or berries, then fresh vegetables, despite their importance, often remain untouched on the plate. And here bright, tasty and nutritious smoothies will come to the aid of caring parents. Smoothies are a great option for children who refuse to eat fresh fruit and vegetables, which are so necessary for the proper development of a growing child's body.

Be careful with your choice of ingredients for making baby smoothies. It is better to choose ingredients familiar to the child: apple, strawberry, or carrot. In the cold season, to strengthen the immune system, you can add cranberries, honey, or cinnamon. But with tropical fruits and citrus fruits, you need to experiment with extreme caution so as not to cause allergies. Do not use store-bought juices to make baby smoothies. The sugar content is too high, even for adults. Try adding fresh juice or good-quality milk.

Once again, we remind you of the need to consult a doctor before introducing new products into your child's diet.

Why are Smoothies beneficial?

Smoothies are tasty, savory, and filled with mesmerizing flavors, but we know all of that already. For almost a century of the development and gaining popularity of smoothies, whole nutrition programs based on smoothies have been developed in the world. These delicious cocktails are included in the diet of almost every person who cares about their health.

But... What are smoothies beneficial for? Why is it worth adding them to your diet? And maybe they have properties that should be treated with caution? Let's figure it out.

To clear up all curiosities, all of these will be discussed here and now in the following chapter. By the time you wrap this chapter up, you will have a comprehensive idea of how much smoothies are valued in our body system.

The value of smoothies lies in their simple and ingenious composition. A smoothie is a concentrate of vitamins and fiber in one glass. Indeed, one portion of a smoothie immediately adds fruits, vegetables, berries, herbs, and superfoods to your diet. From my personal feelings, I can say that eating a smoothie is like recharging your bio-battery. So much vivacity and energy immediately appears!

Smoothies are raw food that take just a couple of minutes to prepare, allowing you to continually experiment with flavors, invent new combinations of foods, and try out unusual ingredients.

How many of us willingly eat the incredibly healthy, yet tasteless hemp protein? And in a smoothie it is easily "overshadowed" by strawberries or bananas, allowing us to get a healthy product without losing taste. The same applies to superfoods - various seeds, proteins, algae, which contain maximum vitamins but are very difficult to integrate into a regular menu.

It is difficult to overestimate the benefits of smoothies for the body. They are a treasure trove of vitamins, including A, C, and K, as well as trace elements, antioxidants, fiber, and sugars, which are essential for strengthening the immune system and the normal functioning of the gastrointestinal tract. In addition, this cocktail is very effective in the fight against excess weight and for maintaining the body with regular exercise. At the same time, you can choose the best smoothie option for you, based on your own needs and taste preferences.

If you include the necessary ingredients and prepare it correctly, this wonderful cocktail satisfies all the body's needs: it maintains muscle tone, increases the level of iron in the blood, is an excellent antidepressant, promotes the production of endorphins, perfectly cleanses the liver, protects against viruses and boosts the immune system, and stimulates hair growth. The green vegetables, chia seeds and flax seeds included in the smoothies improve metabolism and serve as a source of plant-based omega-3 fatty acids. Smoothies can be safely called health elixirs.

Therefore:

15 Reasons to Drink Smoothies Daily

Smoothies give you fresh fruit, vegetables, and berries all year round.

As a rule of thumb, smoothies are always made from unprocessed fruits, vegetables, and berries. They are made from natural products that are still raw and fresh. By happy chance, many studies have substantiated that raw and fresh veggies and fruit are top of the ingredients that you must have in every diet. According to a report by the Harvard School of Public Health, "a diet rich in vegetables and fruits can lower blood pressure, reduce the risk of heart disease and stroke, prevent some types of cancer, lower risk of eye and digestive problems, and have a positive effect upon blood sugar, which can help keep appetite in check." If Harvard School of Public Health has said all of that, what's more to say?

Your body will appreciate fresh over processed food any day.

Veggies are important and there are no two ways about that. If you are one of those who feel disgusted towards fruit and veg, you have nothing to worry about. You only have to consume enough smoothies and you can meet your veggie needs.

Therefore, smoothies are a great way to eat more fresh berries, fruit, or vegetables, and especially greens, at any time of the year - and especially in winter.

Smoothies are the best source of vitamins, antioxidants, and minerals.

One portion of smoothie allows you to fully satisfy the body's daily need for vitamins, minerals, and antioxidants because a smoothie contains many useful ingredients. This is fresh juice, and delicate fruit and berry pectin, and fiber, and all the necessary minerals, vitamins, and biologically active substances, as well as calcium and protein contained in milk.

Due to the grinding of fruits, berries, nuts, and seeds, the cell membranes are ruptured and substances are more easily absorbed by the body, and the presence of several components enhances the effect of the components, which is the miraculous power of smoothies.

Smoothies are simple, fast, and convenient.

Do you have a quick appointment in the early hours but do not want to miss breakfast? Do you need something quick, easy, and tasty enough to make your day? Are you looking to start a busy morning on a quick and healthy fix? Only one answer still comes to mind: smoothies.

Making a healthy cocktail with your own hands will not take you much time. It is enough to have a blender and your favorite ingredients: bananas, apples, pears, apricots, carrots, tomatoes, celery, herbs, and so on. Just put everything in a blender and grind until smooth. The smoothie is ready! And now lack of time is not an excuse for eating wrong.

Smoothies are a great substitute for sweets.

Who says sweets are the most appealing appetizers in the world? It has to be said, sweets are juicy in the mouth, especially when they are additives and condiments. They offer a pleasure that makes you feel like you feel as delighted as a sandboy. Nevertheless, most sweet items contain sugar at precarious levels. You are putting yourself in jeopardy by consuming sugar at high levels.

Rather than depend on sweets, smoothies are a great substitute for you. That is because they are equally delicious, finger-licking, and richer in minerals. They are a conglomerate of ingredients that are not only tasty but are also required by your body. This means, you do not derive pleasure at the expense of your health, it is a win-win on all counts.

If you can't imagine your life without sweets, then smoothies are your drink!

Smoothies are healthy food and health elixir.

Smoothies are a dish that do not produce heaviness in the stomach, and at the same time supply the body with the entire daily norm of minerals and vitamins. Smoothies deliver the nutrients from live food to your body as quickly as possible. Think about it:

29

five minutes ago, the greens were in the refrigerator - boom! - and they're in the stomach already. Crushed foods do not require additional time and energy to chew - they quickly enter the stomach, are easier to digest, and give the maximum amount of nutrients. If you have just switched to a lightweight meal or a vegetarian style, a smoothie will be a perfect addition to your repertoire.

Smoothies are a great way to eat more raw vegetables and especially greens.

Not all people love spinach, celery, parsley, and broccoli, although their benefits are undeniable. Tell me, can you eat, say, a large bunch of parsley, a couple of celery stalks, an apple, and an orange in the morning? And all this at once, chewing thoroughly and for a long time and enjoying the taste? While apples and oranges are easy for me to eat, chewing on a large bunch of parsley isn't very fun. But it's possible with a smoothie. Healthy but specific ingredients such as celery, herbs, or spinach can be added harmoniously to smoothies. In this drink, their specific taste will be masked, but the benefits of these ingredients will be obtained.

Smoothies will help you look younger.

These wonderful cocktails are indispensable for the skin. For dry skin, a cocktail of fresh fruit, vegetables, and berries has a wonderful moisturizing effect from the inside. Those looking for a beautiful and radiant-looking face should include an avocado smoothie in their diet. Several veggies contain carotenoids which protect you from free radicals and harmful radiation that can make your skin age. A study in Japan established that people who ate more green and yellow vegetables tend to develop fewer wrinkles than others who don't. In essence, veggies can make you younger. Also, by regularly enriching the body with vitamins and minerals, your appearance will improve and your skin will be clean and smooth.

Smoothies will help you lose weight.

As highlighted earlier, smoothies are great additions to weight loss plans. You must however ensure you do not get the objective twisted. A smoothie is not originally meant to help weight loss. It is not a diet plan like intermittent fasting, or a low-carb diet, neither is it a weight loss workout plan. It is a casual diet like a Mediterranean diet that can corroborate weight loss plans, and not spearhead it. So, if you consider smoothies as a diet that can contribute to weight loss, your consideration is spot on.

Smoothies are a great way to get rid of toxins.

Toxins are unhealthy junk that got stuck in your blood in one way or another. Many negative factors affect the body every day. We get an unpleasant collection of harmful substances from food, water, and air which tend to accumulate in the body and poison it from the inside. They accumulate in our bodies and cause great harm.

Our body can naturally filter these things out. Our kidneys, lungs, liver, and several other organs in our body have a way of filtering these things. Notwithstanding, you may want to rid yourself of these toxins. You may equally be advised by experts to try some detoxification. Whatever category you belong to, many smoothies can help you detox. To prepare a cleansing smoothie, you need to choose from several ingredients for your smoothie: cabbage, cucumbers, dandelion flowers (during their flowering period), wheat germ, cilantro, parsley, and other herbs. This makes a great detox cocktail. Fiber, which is abundant in smoothies, removes excess toxins.

Smoothies to improve digestion.

Constipation and an upset stomach are quite unpleasant phenomena and most of us face this digestive problem. The crazy rhythm of life makes people constantly rush somewhere, which is why there is often not enough time for a normal and full meal; most replace the necessary meal with tea and a sandwich, and this negatively affects the body. Lack of essential elements, such as fiber, leads to malfunctioning of the stomach. To solve this problem, just throw more vegetables and herbs or fruits and berries into the blender in the morning and mix everything. The intestines will work like a clock. Fiber, dietary fiber, and vitamins will help. Vegetable smoothies (especially if they contain beets) are magical bowel cleaners.

Important! On an empty stomach, you should not eat smoothies made from sour berries or fruit, as well as if you have problems with the gastrointestinal tract.

Smoothies will strengthen the immune system.

If a person's immune system is weakened, then regular colds, fatigue, drowsiness, and irritability will haunt him all the time. Daily use of vitamin smoothies will increase resistance to colds and viral diseases, as well as raise vitality.

A medical study reported by a diet researcher, Natalie Butler, shows that the human immune system requires a lot of vitamins and minerals to keep it going smoothly. She listed citrus, orange, grapefruit, carrot, beet, ginger, apple, tomato, kale, celery, and so forth as foods that can immensely boost the strength of your immune system. All of these can be mashed and processed into a healthy smoothie. In fact, they are, among others, the normal recipes of a smoothie.

Smoothies activate brain activity and improve memory.

To have a good memory and concentration, you need to provide the brain with all the necessary vitamins and minerals. By consuming all kinds of smoothies regularly, we help our brain to cope with the tasks set.

During periods of low blood sugar, smoothies that include banana and coconut can produce medium-chain triglycerides. These can source energy for your brain and help to cut down the tendency of memory loss.

Smoothies help improve sleep.

Another interesting thing about smoothies is that you can tailor them to improve your sleep. If you have trouble sleeping or you needed to ensure that you stay in bed for some time, you can tilt your smoothie to do just that. All you need to do is a sleep-fueled recipe with calcium or milk.

Smoothies are a real antidepressant.

To avoid depression or the blues, make your breakfast bright and positive with colorful smoothies. Smoothies will quickly drive away despondency, and also act as a reliable protector against bad moods. Drinking smoothies seems to return us to a carefree childhood when fruit milkshakes gave us great pleasure.

Green smoothies, kale, spinach, turmeric smoothie, and swiss chard are top reputable smoothies with anti-depressant qualities. As studies have shown, many smoothies contain minerals and vitamins that have anti-depressant qualities, especially vitamin C. This makes them a healthy addition for anyone battling depression.

Smoothies are ideal for athletes

What if you don't have the energy to work out in the gym, and boiled chicken breast only causes an attack of nausea? Try adding smoothies to your diet! They will energize and sweeten a sad diet.

Nutritious and delicious smoothies are essential for active people. Smoothies promote quick energy recovery after workouts, help to strengthen bone tissue, reduce the risk of developing cardiovascular disease, restore muscles and fill the body with useful substances. Such smoothies are called sport smoothies, and you will find them in proper cafeterias.

And now a bonus for those who have children.

Smoothies are a healthy and tasty way to feed your baby

Now, this is the brightest part for babies. As a mom or dad, one of your biggest jobs is to ensure that your kids get all the nutrients they need. While they grow under your watch, they must not be deficient in nutrients and minerals that matter. This can prove to be a herculean task. Children do not eat much and there is a high chance that they'll not consume enough to meet their needs. As a mom, I know how difficult it can be to get a child to eat vegetables - especially green ones.

Rather than keep them in a chair and demand they eat when they are uninterested, you can use smoothies. Simply blend foods that can supply their macronutrients into a smoothie. They can consume all of it without fuss, and they will get all the nutrients you need them to have.

Teaching your child to drink a glass of smoothie in the morning is a wonderful start in life and the best healthy habit you can think of. In the summer, you can freeze smoothies in special tins with sticks and get real ice cream, the benefits of which cannot be compared with store-bought ones.

Make the creation of green cocktails a fun game by letting your child participate.

Start by choosing the right fruit and vegetables from the market together. Instruct your child to wash the ingredients, measure the water, put everything in the blender and, of course, press the button. Let this be your game together. Let the kids experiment a bit on their own and you will see that smoothies will soon become an integral part of their lives.

Disadvantages and Contraindications of Smoothies that You Need to Know About

Many positives for smoothies have been listed. Smoothies are positioned as such a healthy product that some people try to replace all food with them. Why not? Smoothies don't make you gain weight and provide the body with vitamins and minerals ...

But are all smoothies so perfect?

Or do they still have drawbacks that few people talk about? Can the disadvantages outweigh the advantages?

You will get these answers and many other tips in this chapter. This chapter alone can determine what your interest in smoothies should look like.

A smoothie is not a magic drink that can replace entire meals. What harm is there? The dangers fall into two main categories: those associated with making and eating smoothies.

➤ Absurd, but possible: unwashed vegetables and fruit used to make smoothies can cause food poisoning. Therefore, the quality and freshness of fruit and vegetables deserve special attention when preparing smoothies. Buy seasonal fruit and vegetables. This will not only allow you to be confident in the quality and taste but also save you money. Follow simple guidelines for storing food and wash ingredients thoroughly before adding them to your drink.

➢ Cooking at home will guarantee the quality of the smoothie and its ingredients. Therefore, it is better to prepare a drink at home, rather than buy it in cafes or shopping centers. Often, in smoothie bars, sugar is added to drinks in a crumbly form or in the form of sweet juice, syrups, cream, ice cream, which makes the taste of the smoothie sweeter and turns it into a cocktail. Accordingly, the benefits in this case are minimized, and instead of a nutritious meal, you get a glass of unhealthy carbohydrates.

As with any product, smoothies should be consumed in moderation. Otherwise, allergic reactions or digestive upset are possible. Remember the golden rule: nutrition must be balanced. Abuse of any product can lead to negative consequences, and smoothies are no exception. If you abuse smoothies, then you might face the following difficulties:

➢ In large quantities, smoothies can harm even healthy people, as they contain a lot of plant fiber. Because of this, a person may experience colic and abdominal cramps or stool disturbance. The likelihood of such consequences is much higher in those who suffer from gastritis, colitis, and especially ulcers.

➢ Since such a cocktail can be drunk faster than eating all the same fruit in solid form, the brain does not have time to immediately send us a signal of fullness, so this often leads to overeating.

➢ If you completely replace full-fledged food with liquid or puree cocktails, the load on the teeth and gums is significantly reduced. To keep your teeth healthy, you need them to receive a certain load, that is, you need to chew and bite: this stimulates the production of saliva - a natural antiseptic. If there are no chewing movements, then saliva is released in a smaller, insufficient amount, and as a result, the teeth are not fully cleaned with it, bacteria multiply and carry, and other problems develop, for example, plaque.

➢ Thoughtless consumption of smoothies can lead to disruptions in the functioning of the entire digestive system. Liquid food can never replace solid food. Lack of solid food disrupts the gastrointestinal tract and increases the likelihood of constipation. Although there is fiber in a smoothie, fiber alone is not enough to provide the necessary load on the stomach. Therefore, you should not get carried away with smoothies - 1-2 glasses a day are enough.

➤ Fruit smoothies contain a lot of fruit acids, which can also adversely affect tooth enamel. Drinking the smoothie without a straw puts a lot of strain on the enamel of the teeth, often resulting in sensitivity or damage.

➤ With excessive consumption of smoothies, which include dairy components, the level of cholesterol in the body rises significantly and, as a result, problems arise from the cardiovascular system.

➤ One of the contraindications of sugary drinks is both type one and two diabetes since they increase the level of glucose in the blood. In this case, first of all, bananas, grapes, red apples, pears, plums, strawberries should be removed from the list of ingredients. Fruit and berries can be replaced with herbs or vegetables other than beets, carrots, and cabbage.

➤ If you are overweight and especially if you are obese, you should not add fatty milk, yogurts, cream, or ice cream to smoothies. All this will contribute to weight gain instead of weight loss. In this case, it is better to prepare the drink exclusively from herbal ingredients with low-calorie content.

➤ Pregnant women and nursing mothers need to drink such drinks with caution, as they can cause allergies. And, of course, some individuals need to avoid certain ingredients due to intolerance.

And, of course, it is worth mentioning the contraindications. Smoothies are not recommended to be consumed on an empty stomach for people with diseases of the gastrointestinal tract in the acute stage, ulcerative lesions of the digestive system, and diseases and various disorders of the kidneys and liver. In chronic cholecystitis, inflammation of the gallbladder cells may increase with the consumption of smoothies. Start with small portions of smoothies, and avoid citrus and greens as ingredients, as well as hot spices.

Before you start eating fresh vegetables and fruit regularly, you should consult a gastroenterologist.

Rules for Consuming Smoothies

Now that you know the good and bad sides, we need to focus on the binding rules on smoothie consumption. In essence, we need to answer three main questions.

How Often Can I Drink Smoothies?

There are no rules about the number of smoothies you can or cannot drink each day. Likewise, there are no regulations about the size you should consume. You can read different recommendations in different sources. Someone writes that 1-2 glasses of cocktail (250-500 ml) per day will be enough. Someone recommends drinking 1 liter or more smoothies per day. There are many studies and conflicting opinions. The best solution is to try various options and determine what works best for you.

However, you should not get carried away with smoothies so as to replace all meals with them, especially if you go on a strict diet in the form of smoothies. This can have an undesirable effect on the functioning of the gastrointestinal tract. For the intestines to function properly, solid food is needed every day as talked about in the previous chapter.

When Should You Drink a Smoothie During the Day?

Smoothies are most commonly taken as a snack. Plus, a smoothie is an acceptable and reliable breakfast. Sometimes when you're struggling with insomnia, a smoothie can be a great dinner.

Fruit smoothies contain quite a lot of fructose, so it is better to drink them in the morning in order to have time to use up all the energy received from the drink. Green and vegetable smoothies are ideal for an afternoon snack or light dinner.

Buy or Make?

Thick cocktails are offered by many cafes and restaurants; ready-made versions are sold in supermarkets. However, the most delicious and healthy smoothie will be the one you make with your own hands!

Nutritionists around the world claim that it is best to make a smoothie at home. The reason is simple: you know exactly what products go into the finished shake. This, in turn, allows you to change the composition at your discretion, as well as personally control the amount of sugar. The thing is that for a smoothie, the sweetness that fruits and berries give is enough, however, various sweeteners and preservatives are additionally added to store cocktails.

The Perfect Smoothie Formula

The most established idea in this book is that a smoothie is healthy and safe for practically every person. It is made with healthy ingredients and it can supplement certain deficiencies.

With that accepted, we must understand exactly how a healthy smoothie is made. Can you just get the fruit, legumes, and other ingredients and mix them how you like?

Are there specific compositions of each mineral in a healthy smoothie formula? Are there tweaks you should understand and apply when making a delicious and healthy smoothie? Here and now, we have to provide answers to these queries. And we will get started with the right items that go into the correct smoothie formula.

A proper smoothie usually contains three types of ingredients;

> Liquid base
> Base Ingredients
> Natural Additives.

Liquid Base for Smoothies

This comprises all the liquids to be included in the mixture. Most often it is just water, fresh juice (just fresh, not store juice), green or herbal tea, milk, or vegetable milk - from nuts, rice, spelled, sesame or coconut (vegetable milk will give the drink a soft velvety taste, uniformity and make it more satisfying). Very often we use juices, such as citrus fruits, to dilute the fruit or vegetable mass. They go well with most foods, give a slight sourness and sweetness, but they contain quite a lot of sugar, so they should be used carefully, and, of course, it is better if they are freshly squeezed.

Natural yogurt, such as Greek yogurt, can also be used as a base for smoothies. But you can go beyond that by adding syrups, watery fruits, and other things with a similar composition. It is healthier to consider all-natural, and no-sugar options. Some people use coffee when making recipes. However, that could be toxic for children, so you shouldn't consider it if there are kids in the house.

The simplest liquid base option is mineral water, perhaps even carbonated water, which will give the smoothie an airy texture. Do not think that water-based smoothies are not tasty. If the recipe contains sweet fruit or dates, the cocktail will turn out to be quite sweet and tasty. And for vegetable, green, and low-calorie smoothies, water is a good base. It is also better to cool the water beforehand so that the cocktail is not too warm.

A great way to dilute smoothies is to use herbal tea made from linden, mint, lemon balm, chamomile, lemongrass, hibiscus, or raspberry leaf. You can simply chill it or make ice in advance from a brewed herbal mixture.

A properly prepared base is of great importance: if the proportions are not correctly observed, instead of a smoothie, you will get an incomprehensible type of liquid. Try to keep the liquid below 20% volume. Also, make sure your base matches the ingredients you intend to use.

Base Ingredients

Next are the fundamental ingredients. They are the ingredients that you are getting nowhere without. You will have to get them in the right proportions before hoping for a sumptuous product. In almost all cases, your main or base ingredients are fruit and veggies.

The dispute about "what is better to add to smoothies - fruit or vegetables" is about the same as "which tastes better": this, you see, is exclusively a matter of taste. However, nutritionists agree that fruit smoothies are a dessert, not a food. They contain a large amount of sugar (high-calorie), including hidden, give a short-term feeling of fullness, which quickly passes and provokes much greater hunger than before. Drinking a fruit smoothie is like eating cake!

Vegetable smoothies are healthy, but not on their own. This means that by grinding a handful of kale, broccoli, and spinach with water, you only get fiber. To get a balanced smoothie, you need to add the right fats and preferably at least one sour fruit that stabilizes the vitamin C from the greens.

The optimal proportion of vegetables and fruit for a smoothie is 2/3 vegetables, 1/3 fruit, and always a handful of herbs and a spoonful of oil.

This proportion will allow you to get all the most useful nutrients from the drink. Vegetables will give you satiety, fruit - sweetness and taste, plus a little sugar, greens - fiber, all together - vitamins and minerals. And add the rest to your taste - syrups, nuts, superfoods, seeds, sprouts.

Make sure your smoothie is 50% vegetables and fruit.

What could be tastier than a fruity combination? It is the fruit that will give you a charge of vivacity and a good mood!

Here are some types of fruit combinations that work well:

- Banana + apple + strawberry
- Banana +peach + cucumber + salad
- Apple + kiwi + strawberry
- Apple + strawberry + blackcurrant
- Apple + apricot + carrot + spinach
- Banana + pineapple + apple + spinach
- Banana + kiwi + pear
- Kiwi + apple + tangerine
- Pineapple - apple - watermelon
- Papaya - pineapple

Carrots and cucumber are the most frequently chosen vegetables, although almost all vegetables are suitable for smoothies: tomatoes, cabbage, beets, pumpkin, celery, bell peppers, and others. Beets can be taken both raw and boiled.

Here are some fruit & vegetable, and simple vegetable combinations:

- Pumpkin + cinnamon + lemon + grapefruit
- Broccoli + cabbage + celery
- Zucchini + cucumber
- Carrot + ginger
- Apple + cucumber + celery
- Tomato + carrot + apple
- Carrot + celery + apple

- Carrots + beets + cucumber + apple + salad + parsley
- Carrot + apple + cucumber + avocado + spinach
- Apple + bell pepper + salad + pumpkin seeds
- Cucumber + cabbage + pineapple
- Pumpkin + carrots
- Banana + green apple + lettuce
- Banana + pineapple + spinach + avocado
- Mango + cucumber + salad
- Sweet apple + celery + lettuce + spinach + parsley + coconut / almond milk

The best combinations of frozen fruits and berries for smoothies:

- Frozen cranberries + banana + orange juice + sugar + spices
- Frozen cherries + ice cream + honey + cinnamon
- Raspberry ice cream + banana + milk + ice cream
- Frozen strawberries + frozen raspberries + frozen blackberries + frozen blueberries + raspberry juice + lemon juice + milk.
- Any frozen berries + yogurt + honey + spices

Oat flakes:

If you have no issues with oatmeal, then try adding it to smoothies - the number of nutrients and its nutritional value will only increase.

- Milk + oatmeal + bananas + kiwi + strawberries + chocolate + honey
- Milk + oatmeal + honey + dried apricots + raisins
- Oatmeal + banana + orange + natural yogurt + water

Natural Additives

When traditional mixes of fruit and vegetables get boring, the blender is often sent to the back shelf of the cabinet, and the smoothie craze passes. Many common and unusual foods will change and complement the flavor of your usual smoothie. Drink recipes take on a completely different flavor when using additional ingredients.

Natural additives are complementary ingredients that you add to a smoothie. They are not obligatory. They are there to improve the overall taste or quality of the smoothie. They are added in small amounts, up to 5% of the volume. They are seeds, proteins, superfoods, ginger, bee pollen, toppings, decorations, and several others that you add to a smoothie to improve it. Some, like protein and vegetable oils, help you to supplement the minerals and nutrients in the smoothie formula.

Superfoods such as chlorophyll can help increase iron levels in the body. Spirulina or chlorella will saturate us with vitamin B 12 and amino acids. Raw cocoa will give the smoothie a chocolatey hue and flavor, but it is guaranteed to boost your mood by significantly lowering blood sugar. And bright yellow turmeric will help keep you from getting sick during the cold season.

Smoothies made from greens and vegetables can be thickened with chia seeds, they are the record holders for omega-3, 6, and fiber content.

Dry sweet and sour goji berries, rich in fiber and antioxidants, must be soaked in water before use. These berries will give an unusual taste and beautiful color to the cocktail.

Manuka honey and pollen should be added to smoothies after active sports activities - they will relieve fatigue and give vigor, and the Peruvian maca in the cocktail, on the contrary, will calm and bring mood into balance.

Need Fats for a Smoothie?

The right fats are essential for a healthy smoothie. They need to be added - we'll figure out which ones and why.

A unique product for the body is coconut oil, which is sometimes called a superfood. A small spoonful of oil in a smoothie is enough to invigorate. And gaining weight by consuming coconut oil is almost impossible.

The valuable macadam oil has a positive effect on energy levels and skin and hair condition. It is a real beauty oil rich in vitamin E and antioxidants.

Avocado oil can replace a whole range of vitamins: it is high in healthy fats and vitamins. It helps to strengthen the immune system and saturates the body with vitamin A, phosphorus, and iron. And with just two tablespoons of grapeseed oil, you can get your daily dose of vitamin E.

Another very useful oil is flaxseed oil. It has a slightly tart taste, but the benefits compensate for any flavor nuances.

Flaxseed oil will help to fill the deficiency of Omega-3, on which our good mood, vitality, beauty, and thought processes depend.

You can add not only vegetable oil to smoothies but also, for example, ghee. It is easy to digest, has a good effect on intelligence and metabolism, and is lactose-free.

What is the Correct Ratio of Ingredients for a Smoothie?

Here are some simple rules to help you get the best results:

No more than two medium-sized fruit per liter of the finished drink. The fact is that fruits are high in sugar. This is why fruit smoothies are not the best way to start your day. It is necessary to avoid the sharp release of glucose into the blood that happens when eating fruits.

At least three large handfuls of greens or vegetables per liter of the finished drink. What for? It is from these food products that we get the most useful benefits, and it is greens that make such healthy smoothies. If over time you fall in love with smoothies in which there is no fruit at all, then this is only for the benefit of your health. The point, again, is a large amount of fiber, beneficial trace elements, and stabilization of blood sugar levels.

Amount of liquid: all solid ingredients are filled with 2/3 of water or another liquid base.

Fat is a must! To further stabilize blood sugar levels, fat sources should be added to smoothies: vegetable oils, coconut milk/cream, or avocado. For 1 liter of finished drink use: 100 ml coconut milk OR 2 tbsp. any vegetable oil OR 1/2 medium avocado.

Supplements such as ginger, turmeric, cayenne pepper (chili), cinnamon, and lemon are helpful. All of these ingredients have many health benefits. The main thing is not to overdo it with the quantity. For example, for 1 liter of smoothie, I put 3-4 cm of ginger root, 1 small lemon (right with the peel, if you like it). Seasonings - no more than 1-2 teaspoons per liter, otherwise it will be too hot.

Berries are not fruit because unlike fruit they stabilize blood sugar and have a different acidity. So, the good news is that berries can be added to smoothies without restrictions.

How to make a delicious smoothie recipe?

There are different ways to improve the taste of a smoothie. On the whole, smoothies have an appealing taste, especially if bananas, honey, or molasses are included in the ingredients. If you do not have a banana in the recipe, consider adding some ripe and healthy choices.

You should only leave the banana out when it messes up your smoothie composition. In addition to your normal ingredients, you may mix your smoothies with almond milk rather than water. Almond milk is reputably tastier. It contains fewer calories too, making it a smart choice for weight loss enthusiasts. You may equally add sweeteners like honey.

Some helpful tips

Bright berries, such as blueberries, plums, and blackberries, cannot be combined with dark green ones, you risk getting an unappetizing cocktail of an ugly brown color.

For very sweet berries and fruit (such as dates, bananas, and mangoes), it is better to add some citrus fruits or to make them more delicate by adding nut milk.

Pungent vegetables like celery and kale don't pair well with spices like cocoa and cinnamon, although that's also a matter of taste.

If you want to add sweetness to your smoothie, replace the syrups and sugar with dates, prunes, dried apricots, and raw cocoa beans. Even plain vanilla without a gram of sugar will make the taste deceptively sweet.

The more frozen fruits and berries, the thicker the smoothie will be. If you like a softer texture, be sure to cut the rind from the fruit.

Lemon and orange add freshness to the taste and neutralize the taste of the greens. When adding citrus fruits, peel off all films, otherwise, they will taste bitter and will be in the smoothie in the form of chunks.

Peanut butter will make the smoothie more satisfying and add a subtle nutty flavor. For sweet smoothies, use coconut peanut butter, for green smoothies, use salt peanut butter.

Neutral flavored yogurt and avocado pair well with almost any fruit and vegetable, they also add a creamy texture to smoothies and are great for filling.

Very nice and tasty smoothies are obtained with pumpkin, but in pumpkin drink recipes, it is better to avoid harsh additives.

Otherwise, make it the way you like it!

What can be changed for what in a smoothie?

The rules are very simple here: everything is replaced according to the principle of colors. Everything red to red, orange to orange, and green to green. For example, spinach can be easily replaced with parsley or cilantro. Beetroot - bell pepper and apple. Banana -

pineapple ... In general, I advise you to experiment with this, because everyone has different tastes.

How do you replace sugar in smoothies?

Sugar is the most important glue for most people. It is the primary reason they would opt for other smoothies or mocktails that appear to have high sugar content. Sugar isn't encouraged in smoothies; hence, it is replaced by far better alternatives. Common are honey, dates, molasses, and bananas. With the highlighted ingredients, you can get a better taste. You will not recall what sugar tasted like when the natural delicacies melt on your lips.

Can fruit and vegetables be mixed in one drink?

Yes, you can! But smoothies consisting only of fruit are contraindicated. Such a drink is a dessert, not a healthy product. There is too much sugar in the fruit, so save the banana + strawberry + fruit juice smoothie for dessert.

As for the very question of combining fruit and vegetables in one meal, there is no scientific evidence that vegetables and fruits cannot be eaten together. The only thing that you will find on the Internet on this topic is enthusiastic materials from eyewitnesses who will tell you how they began to live better when they stopped mixing fruit with other foods. A better life because their stomach and intestinal discomfort has disappeared. But! Reacting to mixing fruit and vegetables in the same meal is simply a sign that your digestive system is not working properly. If your stomach is swollen, then you should not eat fruit separately, but identify problems with digestion and solve them.

Fruits contain acid and other substances that, on the contrary, contribute to the better digestion of food. For example, natural products that improve digestion are made up of fruit extracts. And pineapple and papaya are even recommended during and immediately after meals to help stomach function.

So mix both fruit and vegetables for health, just make sure that there are at least twice as many vegetables as fruit.

List of Products that Cannot Be Mixed

When consuming smoothies, it is very important not to forget about the rules of food combinations. You don't want your wonderful cocktail to ferment in your stomach, bringing discomfort instead of lightness.

It may sound strange, but some fruit cannot be mixed with certain foods, otherwise, the consequences can be severe for adults and extremely dangerous for children.

Several studies show that these dangerous combinations include:

Pineapple and milk

Pineapples contain bromelain, which can cause serious toxicity when combined with milk or dairy products. Symptoms include nausea, flatulence, headaches, diarrhea, abdominal pain, and even possible infection. It is impossible to give this to a child.

Papaya and lemon

This compound can cause anemia and problems with hemoglobin (blood protein). Especially avoid giving it to children!

Orange and carrots

This is a very popular combination in fresh juices. However, it increases acidity and bile production and damages the kidneys, which can lead to serious illness.

Guava and banana

This combination can backfire.

This leads to the accumulation of gas and acidosis in the stomach, which manifests itself in the form of nausea, heaviness, and pain in the head and abdomen.

Orange and milk

When milk and orange juice mix in the stomach, it makes digestion difficult, especially for children.

Goat or cow milk with fruit/ vegetables

The combination of milk with fruit is an ordeal for the stomach. Cucumbers cannot be combined with cow's milk (by and large, a lot of products cannot be combined with milk).

How to Make a Smoothie: 7 Easy Steps

Everyone can learn how to make amazing smoothies like a true professional. It's not difficult at all! All you need is to master a few basic rules for making this wonderful cocktail once and for all.

Learning how to make a smoothie is very easy if you follow the simple instructions below.

Step 1: Choose a smoothie recipe you like

Let's start, of course, from the very beginning, that is, with the choice of a smoothie recipe. If you plan on consuming smoothies regularly, choose recipes not based on what you have in the fridge or on the shelf, but based on what you expect from this nutritious drink.

Of course, you can make a smoothie with what you have, and this is a normal stopgap measure. However, remember that smoothies can be a delicious "medicine" that can provide your body with tons of nutrients, so feel free to experiment and try to plan your smoothies ahead of time. This way, you always have the right ingredients on hand, and you won't get lost in the thousands of possible recipes and combinations.

So, answer the following important questions:

> ➤ Do you (or whoever you want to share the smoothie with) have a specific diet?
> ➤ Are you allergic or hypersensitive to certain fruits, vegetables, nuts, or commonly used smoothie additives?
> ➤ Do you want to cleanse your body of toxins and lose weight?
> ➤ Looking to saturate your body with protein before or after your workout?
> ➤ Would you like to supplement your diet with fresh fruits and herbs?
> ➤ Do you want to use "smoothie therapy" for disease relief or prevention?
> ➤ Or maybe you just wanted to enjoy a healthy dessert in the form of a smoothie?

The answers to these simple questions will help you decide on the choice of ingredients for your smoothie, and you will know exactly what is right for you to achieve your goal.

If you have no idea for a suitable smoothie recipe that pops up in your head, you can simply search for them in this book. I am sure that you will find something interesting!

Step 2: Add liquid to the blender

The very first step is to pour all of the liquid or semi-liquid ingredients into the blender. Their total amount is usually about 1-2 glasses.

When making your smoothie, try to stick to the suggested recipe and remember that the more liquid you use, the waterier your smoothie will be. Everyone loves a different texture, so act according to your taste. If you like thinner smoothies, you can always add a little more liquid at the end.

A few examples of liquids that I think are great for making tasty and healthy smoothies have been discussed in the previous chapters.

Step 3: Add base ingredients

When we talk about making smoothies, the "base" is what gives the drink its creamy texture.

For a good consistency, I like to add 1-2 bananas to my smoothies. Bananas (fresh or frozen) are a great base that makes smoothies so velvety and delicious.

Other fruits that can act as a base are mangoes, peaches, pears, and apples. Although avocado, coconut pulp, chia seed gel, various nut butters, frozen fruits, and ice can also be used for variety.

But watery fruits such as watermelon, melon, and pineapple, on the contrary, thin the smoothie and greatly affect the consistency, making it less creamy. If you suddenly go too far with them, then a few ice cubes can always come to your rescue, which will quickly and simply help to make the smoothie thicker. This is, of course, a temporary measure, as ice tends to melt quickly, so smoothies filled with ice should be consumed as soon as possible.

Step 4: Add fruits and vegetables

Now that you've decided on your base and liquid, it's time to put the fruits and vegetables in your recipe into the blender. Wash vegetables, fruit, and berries well and, if necessary, peel, remove branches, cores, and stems. Cut large ingredients into small pieces or wedges. Wash and dry fresh herbs well, it is also better to chop them before adding them to the blender bowl.

You can always turn on your imagination and experiment a little. Get creative and enjoy the flavor of a variety of fruit and vegetable combinations. I want to note that you can use almost any fresh or frozen fruits and vegetables to make smoothies. I often add frozen berries to my smoothies, which I use to replace ice, but I prefer to use fruits fresh.

Remember that if you want to make a green smoothie, such as spinach, kale, beet greens, dandelion greens, arugula, or lettuce, you must first chop the greens into small pieces. This is especially important if your blender is not very powerful.
Smoothie recipe ideas can be found in a separate chapter of this book.

Step 5: Additional ingredients

Additional ingredients are the step that will help you improve your smoothie prowess. Moreover, you will get a lot of pleasure from this process.

The numerous ingredients below make a great addition to any smoothie recipe. As you develop your skills in making smoothies, you will intuitively be able to select certain additional ingredients to achieve a certain effect, taste, or consistency.
The Supplement List was not created to overwhelm you - it is intended to inspire new ideas and encourage experimentation.

Sweeteners
Naturally, most smoothie recipes initially include sweet fruits, which add more flavor, but sometimes such ingredients are absent (or there are very few of them) and you need to invent something yourself. In my opinion, the best sweeteners, in this case, are honey, stevia, agave nectar, and maple syrup.

Spice
There is another easy way to play with the flavor and healthiness of your smoothie. This can be done with spices. My favorites include cinnamon, cloves, vanilla, ginger, nutmeg, black pepper, and cayenne pepper. A small amount of these spices and you have almost a new drink with even more active nutrients!

Salt
A small amount of high-quality salt will help make your drink even more healthy and tasty. I prefer Celtic sea salt and pink Himalayan salt.

Superfoods

Today, you can find all kinds of superfoods. They can help boost the nutritional value of your smoothie. Here are a few examples of my favorite superfoods: cocoa (raw chocolate), flax seeds, chia seeds, goji berries, powdered spirulina, coconut products (butter, flakes, pulp), hemp seeds, acai powder, and poppy root.

In addition, there are various highly nutritious green superfoods specially formulated to enhance the nutritional value of smoothies.

Protein powder

If you prefer to drink smoothies after your workout at the gym, then you need something more nutritious with more protein. Protein powder, which can be added to any smoothie recipe, will help you with this.

Step 6: mix everything well

Now that all the ingredients are in place, it's time for the real show. Depending on the type of blender you have and the ingredients you choose for your smoothie, start at light speed and gradually move to a fast speed. If your blender has a special "smoothie" button, then you have nothing to worry about - your miracle machine knows everything by itself.

For example, I like to mix smoothies for 30-60 seconds, depending on the ingredients. However, sometimes it will take several whipping attempts to get the smoothie you want.

Step 7: The most important step in making a smoothie

And now - enjoy its pleasant taste and share this healthy drink with your loved ones!

Smoothies are served either in special glasses with or without handles, or in small bottles. They can be supplied with a lid with a hole for a straw.

And an important rule for the perfect smoothie: you need to drink the drink immediately after preparation! Otherwise, it loses many useful properties.

Key Rules for Making a Real Healthy Smoothie

Everyone can learn how to make amazing smoothies like a true professional. It's not difficult at all! All you need is to master a few basic rules for making this wonderful cocktail. If you stick to these rules and add your ingredients in the right proportions, you are going to achieve a healthy, reliable, and mesmerizing smoothie.

Your smoothies will certainly be better than what is sold in public places, and you can guarantee that it is entirely safe for you and others around you. Here are the key rules to bear in mind when trying to make a healthy smoothie;

Only high-quality components

To make the smoothie tasty, use only ripe and juicy fruit, vegetables, and berries for its preparation. Wash them thoroughly before preparing the drink. Fresh frozen fruit is also suitable for smoothies. Puree from fresh frozen strawberries, blueberries, raspberries, or peaches can create a thick, dense concoction.

Consistency

The correct smoothie will resemble cream, yogurt, or mousse in consistency, the "wrong" - a salad floating in water. It is imperative to add water or another liquid. If this is not done, the smoothie will turn out to be not only too thick but also heterogeneous, that is, it will not live up to its name.

However, adding a lot of water is also not worth it, as the smoothie will turn out to be too liquid, which will affect the taste, and the relative content of nutrients will decrease. If the right amount of water is used, and there are still pieces of greens or fruit floating in the smoothie, then either you turned off the blender too quickly, or it is not powerful enough. By the way, bananas and avocados are great for creating a creamy smoothie texture.

Definition of taste

Before cooking, you should decide on the type of smoothie - sweet, vegetable, or neutral. To prepare a naturally sweet smoothie, you should use products with natural sweetness - berries, bananas, mangoes, or pumpkin. You can also add sweetness with dried fruits (dates, raisins), honey, or natural syrups.

Vegetable smoothies are just as popular as sweet fruit smoothies. As a basis for their preparation, pumpkin, celery, tomatoes, zucchini, or beets are used. You can add some sea salt to the drink. Some people may have a preference for neutral, sometimes even mild tastes. Greens, avocados, and other foods that do not have a pronounced taste are suitable for preparing such smoothies.

Oatmeal is often used to make smoothies. It gives a thick consistency and goes well with cocoa, vegetable milk, fresh and dry fruit, and vegetables. This drink will be more nutritious.

Sweetness

Never add sugar to smoothies - at least if you want a healthy product. Fruit and berry smoothies are sweet enough on their own, but vegetable ones are not. If you have a sweet tooth and can't help but "sweeten the pill", use honey or dried fruit instead of sugar. If the smoothie is too sweet, you can acidify it with lemon or lime juice, or simply add a little water.

Color

As tasty as your smoothie is, its color also matters. In order not to get incomprehensible shades, it is recommended to take products of the same color tone as a basis. For example, you can use a combination of avocado + lime + spinach + kiwi for a green smoothie. Red smoothie: Strawberries, whipped alone or combined with a banana.

You can make a pink smoothie by mixing raspberries with a banana and a little vegetable milk.

An example of an appetizing orange color drink: pumpkin (or persimmon) + peanut milk + honey + a pinch of turmeric (retains the color) + cinnamon. Banana and currant give a pleasant purple hue.

Avoid combinations of ingredients that make it unappetizing. Bright berries, such as blueberries, blueberries, plums, and blackberries, should not be combined with dark greens, do not mix spirulina with strawberries, or blueberries with spinach: you will get a swamp-colored liquid.

Cold but not icy

Note that some blenders will slightly heat the contents of the bowl while mixing. Therefore, if you want a cool drink, it is better to add ice or chilled water from the refrigerator (or frozen berries or a banana) instead of plain water. However, if your blender is not powerful enough, the smoothie may be too cold. In this case, never drink it right away - let it warm up a bit first. Drinks that are too cold are bad for your digestion.

Knowledge of the measure

Experiments are fun and exciting, but too complex combinations do not always lead to success. You should not try to compose compositions from many ingredients: you can get unpredictable tasteless results. Use no more than five ingredients, or even better - three.

The ratio of the components

Use a lot of fruit and veggies: By now, you have caught on to the fact that there isn't much of a smoothie if there are no veggies and fruit. You must, therefore, have a satisfactory amount of fruit and/or veggies in your smoothie.

To make a smoothie not only healthy but also tasty (or vice versa, depending on what you put in first), you need to mix the ingredients in the correct proportions. One of the best options is to use 50% fruits, vegetables, and berries, 30% greens, and 20% liquid. If there is too much greenery or liquid, it can negatively affect the taste. If you overdo it on fruit, your smoothie may end up too cloying, thick, or patchy.

Blender

Don't skimp on your main tool - choose the powerful high-speed option. The resulting mix should be homogeneous. This is one of the main indicators of proper preparation.

Use healthy liquid

A smoothie is not fruit and veggies alone. Other components are as essential as the others. As such, you must guarantee that you are about to use a healthy liquid before using it at all.

To keep your smoothies varied in taste and health, feel free to experiment with different types of liquids. You can use water, plant-based milk (nut, coconut, rice, soy), iced green tea, coconut water, or fresh juice.

Add nut milk instead of cow milk

Important advice: do not use cow's or other milk of animal origin in combination with fruit, otherwise you could cause an unfavorable effect on your body - fermentation, bloating, and even diarrhea. But plant milk goes much better with fruits and herbs, is better absorbed, and makes the drink more beneficial.

Greens

The choice of greens for smoothies is very rich: arugula, parsley, celery, spinach, dill, cucumber, cabbage, and so on. Some don't add greens to smoothies because they don't like the taste, but in small amounts it won't be noticed at all, and you will still get a dose of vitamins and minerals. Natural sweeteners (like the most common banana) also mask its taste. Note: First, it is better to grind the herbs with liquid to the consistency of juice, and then add everything else.

Storage

Usually, smoothies are prepared just before consumption, but in extreme cases, they can be stored in the refrigerator for 24 hours.

Be creative

Where is the fun in a smoothie if you are not doing something crazy every time? As long as you abide by the proper composition and you ensure that your components remain healthy, you can be very creative with your ingredients. You can try making a rainbow smoothie. You may also try a new blend with a different composition.

The most important point is to ensure that the smoothies remain healthy and nutritious.

Color Rules for Smoothies

Color rules are among the most interesting things to learn about smoothies. They are an integral part of what makes smoothies mesmerizing. And they are about how colors should be blended in a recipe to get a beautiful drink.

If you are mixing colors there are several rules and tips you want to remember.

The basic background note is that each color has a different meaning. It has different nutritional information too. Foods of a particular color contain certain trace elements that are similar or interchangeable. For example, all greens are rich in calcium, folate, and chlorophyll (a substance that helps in detoxifying the body). All citrus fruits contain vitamin C and bioflavonoids, which improve the absorption of vitamin C. All oranges contain beta-carotene, which gives the skin a healthy color and protects it from aging.

Hence, it makes complete sense to understand what it is in each color and what it would be missing before blending it with a different color.

So, what are these colors and what can they do?

Fruit colors and their components

Green

Green is one of the colors that can protect against diseases. It supports the immune system, and it efficiently does its job through *Luten*. Green can do a lot more. It is one of the most popular too. Avocadoes, leafy green veggies, peas, and onions are examples.

Orange & Yellow

Working in tandem, these smoothie colors can help to strengthen your immune system too. They contribute to your eyesight and they both contain *beta carotene*. Yellow cabbage, pepper, and carrots are top examples.

White

The peculiar feature of a smoothie is that it can provide essential nutrients that are not available in most other colors. It's not just white, neutral colors may fit this description too. Coconut, pears, apples, and bananas may aptly fill this illustration.

Blue & Purple

These are among the few colors that can contribute to your brainpower. They can strengthen your immune system too. Due to the presence of flavonoids in these colors, they can immensely expand your comprehensive ability and intelligence. Common examples are blueberries, cabbage, and blackberries.

Red

This color is your go-to for a huge improvement in your heart or eye complications. All thanks to the presence of lycopene in the color, it facilitates the eye's ability to focus, capture pictures, and retain information for a while. Watermelon, raspberries, and strawberries are excellent choices.

Having discovered this, you are probably aware that many smoothie makers try to achieve a rainbow with their smoothies. They try to blend different colors so they could have a ray of everything. This isn't wrong, as you now know. You can combine any of these main ingredients and their colors. The most important thing is to focus on their benefits and your body's needs.

What can you replace in a smoothie

The rules are very simple: everything is replaced according to the color principle. Change everything red to red, orange to orange, and green to green.

Why do I recommend replacing ingredients based on the color of your products? It's just that certain colors carry certain trace elements that are similar to each other or are interchangeable. For example, spinach is easy to replace with parsley or cilantro, beets - bell pepper or apple, banana - pineapple ... In general, I advise you to experiment. Everyone has different tastes, and only you can choose the optimal combination of products for yourself.

However, as you experiment with recipes, keep in mind that combining ingredients of certain colors can make the drink look unappetizing. In particular, a combination of berries and greens like spinach can give smoothies a marshy green hue. This may not spoil the taste of the drink, but your desire to drink it may disappear.

Common Smoothies Errors and Ways around Them

Mistakes happen in everything. It is human to make mistakes especially if you never went to study how it is done in a college and got grades. You tend to do it the way it pleases you.

Sometimes, you assume it is all creativity. Likely, you're not far off. But we must accept the fact that some creativities are not necessarily right. If not, you may be putting yourself at risk of health complications or selling short the quality of your smoothie. So, what are these errors?

Under-blending or not blending enough

Smoothies don't take time to blend. But you should not be too brief about it. Ensure it properly blends before turning the blender off. 30s is not enough. 2-3 minutes can do it. You should even give it a bit more if necessary.

Too frothy smoothie

Try adding less water to the smoothie next time or not whisking it for too long. If you are afraid to overdo it with liquid ingredients, then you can pour in a little until you get the desired consistency.

A thickening base, namely the ingredients listed above (banana, avocado, coconut pulp, chia seed gel, peanut butter, yogurt, frozen fruit, and ice) may also help in this situation.

Milk often leads to an excessive frothiness in the drink, so it can be replaced with apple juice or plain water. When making smoothies with greens such as spinach, you don't need a lot of liquid, since these ingredients already contain enough water.

Ice

There has been debate on the value of ice over the years. Is it really good for our health or has it got some devastating complications? There is no final answer. But at the least, excess ice cubes can make it difficult for some ingredients to melt and blend into the mixture. So, don't use too much.

Stuffing an arsenal in the smoothie

Hey! This isn't a free for all. You wouldn't stick everything in your kitchen in a rice or quinoa dish. This isn't very different. You must see it that way, at least. It is important to pick only a few ingredients and stick to them.

Overstuffing your smoothie with the wrong stuff

Now, this is something that should be taken seriously. More than half of the time, some condiments, additives, and artificial sweeteners appear so good that you're prompted to add more than a sufficient amount of them. Several other ingredients are just like this. You should understand, however, the more you add, the more you destroy the quality of your smoothie.

The smoothie is not tasty or too savory

This problem is usually very easy to solve by adding more sweetness to the smoothie. You can use any sweetener you like. For example, I prefer natural honey or maple syrup.

Alternatively, for extra sweetness, you can use dried fruit, a banana, or a ripe, juicy pear. Usually, these ingredients help to correct the taste of even the most tasteless smoothie.

Excess sugar

Some people think that a smoothie must all be yummy and mesmerizing in the mouth. Of course, this is not wrong, and a blend between high and low-sugar fruits can achieve it. But that's not it for a lot of people, particularly restaurants and smoothie kit sellers. They go overboard and add anything that can increase the appeal of the smoothie on your lips. Not healthy, you must understand. You should not even add excess high-sugar fruits just to get a mesmeric taste. The taste isn't permanent, the health effect can be, so pay attention to that more.

Not using a thickener

Who says thickeners are bad? You're bastardizing your smoothie if, through all these years, you've never used a thickener. Apart from using thick foods like apricots, mangos, and peaches, you can mix chia seeds and bananas to achieve thickness.

Using the wrong fruits

We agreed you are using fruit, and that's what most people accept. The other part that they are not getting right is that you are using just any fruit that appears on the table. It must not be ripe to the point that it rots. It should neither equally be underripe. You're not going to get the right nutrients, the right taste, and the right impression in either case.

Using all the liquid at once

This often happens in big and busy cafeterias. The caterers understand that there is a large crowd waiting and they try to get things done as quickly as possible. So, they pour all the liquid in at once, then stir the ingredients. Unfortunately, it doesn't always work that way. Ideally, half of the liquid should be used to mix and blend first. The other half should seep into the mixture halfway as it thickens. You can even add some when it is all done.

Smoothies don't mix well

This means that you are using too little liquid. If you fill the blender bowl too compactly, mixing may be difficult. Remember that the blender blades must be completely covered with liquid. In the beginning, I often made this mistake and then I had to poke around in the ingredients to push them below. So, if there is not enough liquid in the blender to unwind its knives, you can add a little more liquid. This will immediately start the mixing process.
Moreover, if your blender is not very powerful, it is best to cut the fruit and other ingredients into smaller pieces.
If you plan to add ice to the smoothie, but you have a weak blender, then first mix the liquid with fresh fruit and vegetables, and only then add the ice and frozen fruit.

Being uncreative

We have got to say this too. By choosing to stick to the smoothie recipe you got from a dietitian or your friend, you are making a terrible mistake. You are selling yourself short. There is no final tried-and-true method in the smoothie enterprise. It is all fun. You need to do something weird, try a different blend, tweak the customs a little bit, and see how it comes out now and then.

Don't neglect your food groups

Different food groups must be encountered - proteins, grains, and several other classes. You have calcium, vitamins, among others that need to be supplied. It is important to book an appointment with a dietitian and figure out what needs to be upped in your diet and what needs to be moderated. That way, you don't stuff the wrong things using the right process. Fair warning, never store your smoothie for too long. Preservatives are not great ideas either.

Did the smoothie end up on the walls and ceiling of your kitchen?

Yes, that happens too.

Perhaps this advice will seem ridiculous to some, but for others, it can be salvation from cleaning the kitchen. So, ALWAYS make sure the blender lid is tightly closed. Once I closed the blender bowl loosely with the lid and turned it on at full power. As luck would have it, this smoothie was pretty runny and I splattered the smoothie all over the place. Fortunately, the walls of our kitchen are tiled, and it was quite easy to clean them. Nevertheless, I have learned this lesson and now I check the lid several times before starting the blender or even hold it with my hand at all times until the smoothie is ready.

How to Choose an Ideal Blender for Smoothies

Having a good blender is similar to having a superfast car that can travel a mile a minute. You know that no matter what you choose to blend, you are always prepared. Without a good blender, however, you will always find particles in your smoothie and that might reduce the pleasure.

You'll feel like you are eating the content of the mixtures one after the other, rather than eating all of it at once. So, you need to choose the right blender. First, what are the top features you should look out for when buying a blender for smoothies and shakes?

Features of a good smoothie blender

> It should have a large container.
> The container should be of high quality, preferably, stainless steel. Glass is an environmentally friendly material, but the jug will be heavy and there is a risk of breaking it.
> Ensure the blades and the drive sockets are stainless steel.
> The blade socket should be easy to replace
> Ensure that there is a pulse button to break up veggies and crush ice.
> The blender should have a speed controller.
> Your blender should be able to change food settings. You should have different options for stirring, chopping, mixing, and so forth.
> Your blender should be high-powered, anything from 300- 1,300 watts.

Types of blenders

1. **Hand mixers:** the names tell it all. They are simple to use and can be electric. They do not have many uses. Mostly, they blend ingredients. They are good for bakers and people who don't have to chop ingredients to small bits and water, never smoothie makers.

2. **Single-Serve Blenders:** Single-serve blenders are the ideal smoothie blenders. You can make pancakes, omelets, and pureed food with them too. They are quick and you don't get exposed to the blade while it is working. The downside is that some of them leak, and most others are not designed to blend hard stuff like chia seeds. Sometimes, the blades don't come off again.

3. **Immersion and Stick Blender:** these are pretty common. They are easy to move around and quite flexible. Immersion blenders are used to blend soups and liquids. That makes them a good option for smoothies too. They are handheld, and easy to move around, unless they are cordless.

4. **The countertop blenders:** these are the typical family blenders. They are large, difficult to move around, and powerful. They are made of high-performance motors which makes them heavier than average. It makes them multipurpose too. If you are preparing a lot of smoothies, the countertop is a great choice.

5. **The full-size blenders:** these are the master blenders. They are the complete version of everything a blender could be. Larger than the countertop, they are on the high side and they have remarkably broad containers. With impressive blades, full-size blenders are capable of grinding ingredients. They can be used but they are not the best.

It is believed that for making smoothies it is better to use a stationary blender rather than an immersion blender: this way you will achieve a more uniform texture of the finished drink. On the other hand, a hand blender with a special attachment does a better job of chopping dry ingredients like nuts or dried fruits.

By and large, none of the blenders are bad. But you have to consider the one tailored to suit your needs when selecting a blender for smoothies. In particular, you need one that can crush the sort of ingredients you will use when making recipes.

What should you look for when buying a blender?

The jar capacity of the blender

The higher the capacity, the easier it is to mix things in it. Anything between 0.7 Liters and 2 Liters is excellent.

The quality of the blade

Stainless steel blades are smart choices. They offer a diamond cut and are easy to operate. You can easily tell by glancing through the features and product description.

Portability

Sometimes, you need something you can shuffle between your bags and move from home to work. You might need something you can travel with or drop in your bag when you're visiting friends and you're looking to make smoothies for them. When this is the case, you should get a portable blender. On the flip side, you may need something that can be easily used by the kids or your friends when they come over. In that case, a less portable blender works better.

The power of the blender

You are going to be crushing bananas and oranges, not rocks and trees. There may be no reason to purchase an extremely powerful blender, especially if you have another blender for much harder stuff.

If you have no other blender and you are trying to be insightful, however, you need a strong blender. You do not want to have a blender that's no use other than for smoothies. It can be exasperating to have a blender you can't use when you need to get some other things crushed. The worst part, you might be prompted to use the blender to crush harder objects. In the process, the blades can break and the blender could be ruined.

Keep your eye on noise dampening blenders

Due to the mechanical activities running in it, an average blender makes a whole lot of noise. That noise can damage your ears if you are exposed to it for too long. You may want to consider the level of the noise alongside other factors.

You should know, the higher the power of a blender, the higher its tendency to be noisy. Some high-quality blenders have been made to suppress their noises despite their capacity. That's what you should look for.

Despite these subtleties, power should remain the main criterion when choosing a blender, and the principle "more is better" works here, especially if you prefer to add a lot of ice to your cocktails. And of course, do not forget that, like any household appliance in the kitchen, a blender requires special care: disassemble it before washing to prevent the accumulation of bacteria on various parts of the appliance.

FAQ about Smoothies

I am allergic to bananas (pineapples, peaches, etc.), what can replace them?

There is nothing wrong with you at all. Let's begin from there. Empirical studies indicate that one of six persons has close to no interest in fruit at all. If you are one of those, you are normal and you do not have to fill your smoothie with what you seemingly loathe. Rather than use fruit, try canned pumpkin, frozen fruit and veggies, coconut cream sweet potato, chia seeds, yogurt, and avocado.

How to achieve a smooth, creamy consistency?

a. Always remember to add health boosters like chia and flax seeds.
b. Mix your ingredients with half the liquid at first.
c. Wrap it up with the other half.
d. Allow it enough time to blend.
e. Add some yogurt if it doesn't wreck the blend
f. A few spices and powders to keep things glued.

I love sweet smoothies. How do I sweeten my shake?

You do not always have to mix a sweetener with your ingredients, particularly if you have banana and lemon in it. If you'd like some sweeteners, however, a few are acceptable. You can try maple syrup, honey, or agave.

Is it better to buy or make your smoothies?

Smoothies bought outside can save you the trouble of mixing, stripping, or cutting ingredients. But that's the only advantage. You do not have to buy the ingredients individually either, especially if some would go to waste because you only need a little.

Nevertheless, it must be said that ready-made smoothies are often poorly made. They are excessively spiced with sugar and sweeteners and generally unhealthy for you. It is worst when you're making smoothies for weight loss or other specific health reasons. Your best option remains to make the smoothies yourself. It is fast, easy, and inexpensive.

What container is the best for storing smoothies?

The best containers you can use are closely sealed (airtight) glass containers. If you can, fill them to the brim to avoid air being trapped and contamination. It can be managed if it isn't filled to the brim too.

How long can smoothies last?

Smoothies shouldn't be kept for more than two days. They are super easy to make. You shouldn't make it till you need it, and you shouldn't make excess.

What to do if you are not full from smoothies

If your smoothie doesn't fill you up, you are probably not using the right ingredients. Try frozen fruits, nut butter, flax/ chia seeds, nut butter, greens, whole grains, and yogurt. You should not make enough to get drunk. But you should be satisfied especially if this is your meal.

What to do if your belly swells after a smoothie

First, you should reduce your intake of cruciferous veggies. That includes kale, cabbage, and broccoli. Reduce your intake of beans, kefir, and watermelon too. Turn to mild foods like avocado and sweet potatoes. Banana is an option too. And drink enough water.

Can you lose weight on smoothies?

Yes! A smoothie can fast-track your detoxification which contributes to healthier digestion. It can in turn lead to weight loss. There are regular smoothie recipes that can lead to weight loss.

Is "liquid food" bad for your teeth and stomach?

According to the director of clinical operations at Texas A&M University Baylor College of Dentistry, Cherri Kading, "tooth decay and erosion of tooth enamel are the biggest concerns associated with liquid diets." So, consuming an overly liquid diet may cause decay particularly if you have added natural sugar or unnatural sweeteners.

Is it true that smoothies don't have complete fiber? And is it worth enriching them with protein?

A smoothie provides as many nutrients as available in the source ingredients. In other words, you will get all the nutrients domiciled in fruit, veggies, seeds, or any ingredient you use for a smoothie. Since fiber is largely deposited in fruit and veggies, it is not lost in the blending process. So to sum up, you get complete fiber in your smoothie.

Often, it is healthy and smart to boost your smoothie with protein. This is because most smoothie ingredients run low on protein, and it has to be supplemented, especially if this is going to be a full meal.

Smoothies for Breakfast

Smoothie Tropical Breakfast

I suggest you prepare a wonderful dish today - a breakfast of banana, tangerine, and coconut with oatmeal in a jar. Perhaps such a breakfast is something completely unusual for you, but believe me, it is worth trying it once, and you will want to make it over and over again.

Ingredients

1 banana
2 tangerines (or 1 orange)
1 tablespoon oatmeal
1 tablespoon dried dates
1 tbsp. l. coconut flakes

1 teaspoon of flaxseed
1 teaspoon sunflower seeds
1/2 cup natural or soy yogurt

How to Make

Dry the oatmeal in a dry skillet (over low heat) for 2 minutes. Peel the tangerine (or orange), cut it into pieces, remove the seeds from the pulp. Pour hot water over the dates and let them absorb some moisture, 5 minutes is enough. If there are seeds in the dates, remove them.

Mix the banana, tangerine, or orange slices and dates in a blender, add the coconut and yogurt. Whisk the breakfast ingredients for 2 minutes.

Place ¾ of the oatmeal in a breakfast bowl, drizzle over the smoothie, sprinkle with the remaining oatmeal, sunflower seeds, and flaxseeds. Put the dish in the refrigerator for 20 minutes to allow the oatmeal to absorb the fruit juice and yogurt. Then remove the breakfast from the refrigerator and serve immediately. Bon appetit and have a nice day!

Berry & Pomegranate Smoothie

This refreshing berry breakfast smoothie is loaded with vitamins and organic acids. Chia seeds make it very satisfying, saturating the body with fiber, omega-3 fatty acids, calcium, and other beneficial elements.

Ingredients

1 cup Berry Mix (raspberries, blueberries, strawberries)
1/2 cup Sugar-free pomegranate juice
1/2 cup Water (you can add a few ice cubes for coolness)
1/2 tbsp. l Chia seeds
mint leaves for decoration

How to Make

Squeeze out the pomegranate juice (or use a ready-made one). Prepare the berries - wash, remove the stalks (berries can frozen).

Add the berry mix and pomegranate juice to the blender bowl and stir until smooth. Then add the chia seeds and stir. Add water in portions to the consistency you need.

Whisk all of the ingredients in a blender.

If you used a fresh berry mix, you could add a few ice cubes to keep the smoothie cool.

Pour the smoothie into beautiful glasses and enjoy!

Banana & Sweet Cherry Smoothie

For a delicious family tradition for breakfast or snack, try making a healthy sweet cherry drink. Sweet cherries are low in calories and very healthy. Unlike cherries, sweet cherries do not cause heartburn, so they can be consumed even by people with high stomach acidity.

To make the fruit smoothie more satisfying, I added natural yogurt, and for the aroma and more delicate taste, I decided to use a ripe banana. It turned out so delicious that I decided to freeze some of the berries so that in winter I could enjoy the sweet cherry smoothie again.

Ingredients

1 banana
a handful of sweet cherries
1/2 cup natural yogurt
mint leaves (for decoration)

How to Make

Peel a banana that has been pre-chilled in the freezer. For easy chopping in the blender, cut into rings. Wash the cherries and remove the seeds.

Combine the fruits in a blender. Add cold yogurt. It is advisable to use a naturally fermented milk product to get the maximum benefit.

Whisk the ingredients at high speed until smooth. Pour the smoothie into pretty cups and garnish with a sprig of mint.

Smoothie with Pineapple, Dates, and Peanuts

A very interesting taste is obtained if you combine the pulp of pineapple, orange, add dried dates, and slightly fried peanuts.

Smoothies made from dates turn out to be quite sweet and do not require any additional sweeteners, and since peanuts are used in the recipe, it is also amazingly satisfying.

The drink has an excellent taste, is surprisingly healthy, and incredibly invigorating. This smoothie is quick and easy to make, and the perfect breakfast is on the table in front of you in seconds.

Ingredients

1/2 cup pineapple chunks (fresh or frozen)
1/2 orange
6 pieces of dried dates
1 teaspoon of poppy seeds
2 tablespoons of peanuts
1/2 cup natural yogurt

If you are using fresh pineapple, then cut it, free it from the top layer, and chop the pulp into small cubes.

Peel the orange, also cut into small slices, if possible, get rid of the seeds. Remove the pits from the dates.

Put the pineapple pieces, orange slices in a blender container, add the dates, peanuts, and poppy seeds. Pour yogurt over everything. Turn on the blender for 30-40 seconds and when the smoothie is ready, all there's left to do is pour it into glasses.

Smoothie Poppy Surprise

This recipe for a yogurt and poppy seed smoothie is very simple and will not take you more than five minutes.

My new drink looks very interesting: the black dots of the poppy seeds contrast perfectly with the white background of natural yogurt. I usually do not add walnuts to smoothies in the blender, but grate them on a fine grater and decorate the drink with nut crumbs. It turns out very nice and convenient: if you want, eat a nut slide, scooped up with a spoon, or if you want, mix with a smoothie.

Ingredients

1 cup natural yogurt
1 tsp poppy seeds
1 tsp fresh honey
1 tsp chopped walnuts or hazelnuts
1/2 apple

How to Make

Peel half of the apple, remove the core and cut into several small pieces. Place the apple slices in a blender, add yogurt and fresh honey.

Whisk the ingredients at high speed for 1 minute.

Open the blender lid and pour the poppy seeds into the smoothie. Stir the drink with a spoon to distribute the poppy evenly in it.

Grate walnuts or hazelnut kernels on the shallow side of the grater or grind them in a coffee grinder.

Pour the finished yogurt and poppy seed smoothie into a glass, sprinkle with nut crumbs, and serve. Bon Appetit!

Banana, Avocado, and Hempseed Smoothie

A quick smoothie with lots of good fiber and greens ... This smoothie is packed with many nutrients - healthy fats from avocado, phytonutrients from spinach, potassium from the banana, and omega-3s from hemp seeds. This creamy pear, avocado, and hemp smoothie are sure to spice up your weekend!

Ingredients

    1/2 large avocado
    1 ripe banana, frozen
    1 ripe pear, peeled
    1 sweet apple, chopped
    1/4 cup parsley
    1 cup kale or greens of choice (spinach, collards, and chard)
    1 1/4 cups almond milk
    1 teaspoon lemon juice
    1 tablespoon flax seeds

How to Make

To start, place all of the ingredients needed to make the smoothie in a high-speed blender. Blend it for 2 to 3 minutes on a low speed or until smooth. Next, blend it again for another minute at a high speed or until frothy. Finally, transfer to a serving glass and serve immediately.

Strawberry Yoghurt Smoothie with Pistachios

I would like to suggest that you prepare a very tasty drink based on strawberries and yogurt with delicious pistachios. Whatever the season, be sure to try this smoothie. In summer, you can use fresh berries, and in winter, frozen strawberries are perfect for making a drink.

Ingredients

1/2 cup fresh or frozen strawberries + 1 strawberry for garnish
1 teaspoon chopped pistachios
1/2 cup natural or soy yogurt
1 teaspoon honey or any other natural sweetener
1/5 cup apple or strawberry juice

How to Make

If using fresh strawberries, rinse them in cool water and remove the stalks. Remove frozen strawberries from the freezer 10 minutes before smoothing.

Peel the pistachios and rub the kernels between your palms to get rid of excess husks.

First, place the pistachios in a blender bowl and chop until they are coarse - about 30 seconds. Open the lid and pour the nut crumbs onto a plate. Now stir the strawberries into the blender, add yogurt, sweetener, and juice. Whisk the ingredients well for 2 minutes.

Pour the finished smoothie into a glass, sprinkle with pistachio chips and garnish with strawberries. Insert a cocktail tube into your drink and start tasting. Bon Appetit!

Dried Fruit & Walnut Smoothie

In the cool season, when the body suffers from a lack of trace elements, dried fruit can become a source of nutrients. Sometimes I recommend pampering yourself with a dried fruit smoothie, which will not only replenish the missing vitamins but also saturate you with energy for the day.

Ingredients

1 tablespoon of dates
1 tablespoon of dried apricots
1 tbsp figs
10 pcs prunes (dried or smoked)
Raisins 20 1 tbsp
Walnuts 1 tsp
1 glass of milk
3 tbsp. l. oatmeal
spices: ginger, cinnamon, or cardamom (optional)

Separate the dates from the seeds. If the figs, dried apricots, and raisins are hard, soak them in warm water for 10 minutes to soften a little, then rinse. Prunes have a rather pronounced taste, so do not add too many, so as not to overpower the taste of the rest of the dried fruit.

Use a sharp knife to cut the dried fruit into small pieces and put it into a blender or food processor. Grind the nuts separately in a coffee grinder (food processor) or crush them in a mortar to a medium crumb, add to the dried fruit.

First, whisk the dried fruit and nuts with a little milk in an impulse blender for 30 seconds. Then mix the half-whipped mass with the rest of the milk and beat as usual. With this mixing, the pieces of dried fruit and nuts are crushed to the maximum. But if you like the presence of large particles, you can immediately combine the components with all of the milk.

Then you can add oatmeal and, if desired, add one of the suggested spices, as well as a small amount of crushed ice for cooling. Beat the mixture again, pour into glasses, garnish with raisins. I ended up with a thick fluffy smoothie that needs to be eaten with a spoon. To avoid this, you can add more milk or ice.

Smoothie with Persimmon, Pumpkin, and Nuts

I especially love this smoothie. I associate it with cool autumn days when everything around becomes golden and crimson from yellowed foliage on trees and shrubs.

Ingredients

1 large banana
1 cup shredded raw pumpkin
1 large persimmon
a handful of walnuts

Choose a pumpkin that is sweet and ripe with a bright, rich orange hue for this smoothie.

Prepare the pumpkin: cut off the stem of the pumpkin and cut the vegetable in half and remove the seeds (they can be washed, dried, and then fried in a dry frying pan. The seeds can be used as a healthy snack or added to smoothies, soups, pastries, and other dishes). Peel the pulp and cut it into small pieces of any shape. This will make it quicker and easier to grind the pumpkin in a blender.

Peel the banana and break it (or cut it into rings). Remove the stalk from the persimmon, if any. Cut the fruit into several pieces. If there is a stone, then it must be removed.

Now combine the necessary ingredients. Grind the banana and persimmon. Pour all the pieces of fruit into the blender bowl. At the maximum speed of the blender, turn them into a smooth and thick puree.

Next, add the pumpkin seeds and walnuts to the resulting fruit mixture with the pieces of fresh pumpkin. Kernels can be added whole or pre-minced in a blender or chopped with a knife.

Mix all of the ingredients in a blender again, achieving a homogeneous mass with a smooth texture.

Pour the smoothies into glass cups or special smoothie jars. "Stick" a cocktail tube into each smoothie and sprinkle the drink with chopped nuts.

Optionally add a pinch of cinnamon and crushed ice to the smoothie.

Tofu Banana Vanilla Smoothie

This creamy smoothie will appeal to both vegans and healthy smoothie lovers alike. It does not contain animal products but contains highly digestible proteins and other nutrients.

Ingredients

1/2 cup Soft tofu
1 cup Vanilla soy milk
1 Banana
1/2 tbsp. l. Peanut butter

How to Make

Chop the tofu. Peel the banana and break it (or cut it into rings). Put them in the blender bowl. Whisk them with butter and milk in the blender.Pour the smoothie into beautiful glasses and enjoy!

Savory Strawberries Blueberries Smoothie

Ingredients

1 cup Blueberries, frozen
1 cup Strawberries, frozen
1 cup Rolled Oats
1-inch Ginger, chopped roughly
2 tbsp. Almond Butter
2 cups Baby Spinach
One ¼ cup Water
3 tbsp. Hemp Seeds, hulled
2 tbsp. Maple Syrup

How to Make

First, put all of the ingredients needed to make the smoothie in a high-speed blender. Blend for 2 minutes or until the mixture is smooth and creamy.

Tip: You can use sunflower seed butter instead of almond butter.

Pear & Walnut Smoothie

The juicy pears and walnuts combination, lightly sweetened with a drop of aromatic honey, can be drunk any time of the day simply because it tastes good.

But the benefits of this smoothie don't end there. If you are a little dissatisfied with your weight and a small correction in this regard will cheer you up, then a pear smoothie according to this recipe will be very useful. It perfectly fills the stomach, and at the same time, the feeling of hunger completely disappears. It is important to strictly adhere to the specified recipe, that is, without sugar and chocolate. Only a slight increase in the amount of honey is allowed for "chronic" sweet tooths.

Ingredients

1 pear
1 tablespoon walnuts, shelled and chopped
1 cup natural yogurt without fillers (can be substituted for soy yogurt)
1 tablespoon honey or any other sugar substitute

Tips. When choosing products for this smoothie, remember that pears must be of very juicy varieties. Since my pears are quite large, one was enough for me.

How to Make

First, let's prepare the nuts. If you have a weak blender or do not like small chunks of nuts in a smoothie, then you need to grind the peeled nuts into flour. To do this, you can use a conventional coffee grinder. If the blender is powerful enough, you can put the peeled nuts in without pre-processing or chopping.

Next, pour the yogurt into a blender bowl.

Cut the pear into small cubes and add the pieces to the yogurt.

Add the chopped nuts and a tablespoon of natural flavored honey (or another sweet substitute).

Turn the blender on full power and beat until smooth.

Pour the contents of the blender bowl into tall glasses and serve.

Hearty Fruit Chia Smoothie

I want to share with you my favorite breakfast smoothie recipe. For me, breakfast is the most important meal of the day, so I like it to be healthy and satisfying. So, our hearty smoothie consists of basic fruits (apple, banana, and pear), natural yogurt, and a few tablespoons of chia seeds and flax seeds.

If you don't have chia, then you can replace them with a tablespoon of regular oatmeal. It also turns out tasty and satisfying.

Remember that flax seeds need to be used ground because they have a very tough shell, which our body simply cannot dissolve. I usually grind flaxseeds in a coffee grinder.

Ingredients

1 banana
1 pear
1 apple
1 glass of natural yogurt
2 tbsp. l. chia seed
2 tbsp. l. flax seeds (ground)

Pour the yogurt into a blender bowl.

Peel the banana, break or cut into pieces, and put into a bowl of yogurt.

Wash the pear and apple well, remove the core and seeds, and cut into pieces. If you do not like small particles of peel in smoothies, then the fruit can be pre-peeled from the top layer. Then, add the apple and pear to the rest of the ingredients.

Finally, add the chia seeds and pre-shredded flaxseeds, and turn the blender on at full power. Whisk until smooth.

Pour the smoothie into beautiful glasses and enjoy!

Advice:

If at the end the smoothie turns out to be too thick, then it can be slightly diluted with yogurt or cold water.

Vegetable Smoothies for Lunch and Dinner

Savory Cauliflower-Garlic Smoothie

You might be thinking that cauliflower and garlic smoothies would not be delicious, but you are wrong. Quick, easy, and delicious, this savory smoothie will satisfy your appetite and your daily serving of vegetables at the same time.

Ingredients

    2 cups cauliflower flowers
    2 cloves of garlic
    1 glass of Greek yogurt
    1 glass of water
    1 glass of ice

How to Make

In a blender, combine the cauliflower, garlic, yogurt, and ½ cup water with ½ cup ice and beat until smooth.

While stirring, add the remaining water and ice until the desired consistency is achieved.

Zucchini & Greens Smoothie

If you want to surprise your guests with an unusual drink or diversify your diet, you can make a zucchini smoothie. This light dessert is especially popular with dieters. It tastes good on its own and when combined with other fruits, vegetables, and even berries.

Ingredients:

1 zucchini and 1 cucumber
1 tsp lemon juice
a couple of dill sprigs
6-8 fresh mint leaves
½ tsp liquid honey (if thick, melt in a water bath)

How to Make

Peel the vegetables from their tails, wash, dry. If the zucchini is young, you cannot peel the peel, and if you're in doubt about its purity, wash it with soda. Also, process the cucumber. Rinse the dill and mint, shake to remove any excess moisture. Chop finely.

Pour the vegetables and herbs into a blender. Pour everything with a little lemon juice, and then honey. Close the lid and grind everything until smooth. The drink is immediately ready to serve. Additionally, ice cubes can be added for a more refreshing taste.

Remember to insert the wide drinking straws.

Carrot & Celery Smoothie

This is a wonderful and super healthy carrot and celery smoothie. Since celery has a rather bright taste and bitterness, I suggest adding honey to taste, I needed 1 tbsp. To prevent the smoothie from turning into just a vegetable/fruit puree, a liquid component is usually added: milk, water, juices, etc. I usually add orange juice.

Ingredients

Petiolate celery - 2-3 stalks
Carrots - 1 pc
Orange - 1 pc
Honey - to taste

How to Make

Grate the carrots on a fine grater, put them in a blender.

Cut the celery stalks across into thin slices. You can also add delicate greens. Grind the vegetables in a blender, you get a rather thick mass.

Add the juice of one orange and honey. Beat the mass again. Taste and add more honey if needed. So our wonderful carrot and celery smoothie is ready. Pour the drink into glasses and enjoy the great taste.

Broccoli, Apple & Lime

Broccoli smoothies are very healthy and low in calories. Such a composition acts as a cleansing agent on the body, accelerates metabolic processes, and also improves the functioning of the gastrointestinal tract. This recipe perfectly disguises broccoli and is especially suitable for those who do not like the smell of cabbage.

Ingredients

5-6 broccoli florets
1 green apple
½ lime
1 cup mineral water (cold)

How to Make

Divide the washed raw broccoli into florets (can be boiled), transfer to a blender bowl. Peel the apple, remove core, and tail. Leave the peel as desired. Cut the lime in half, remove the seeds, squeeze the juice. Transfer to a blender. Add mineral water.

Grind the ingredients for 1 minute on the maximum blender setting. Pour the drink into glasses and drink immediately.

Broccoli & Lettuce Smoothie

This vegetable drink will brighten up a light breakfast and put you in a positive mood. The ingredients will give away their useful substances to the maximum, and together with the zucchini, they will create an incredible, slightly specific flavor combination.

Ingredients

1 zucchini
1 cucumber
5-6 broccoli florets
4-5 lettuce leaves
yogurt to be diluted (if needed)

How to Make

Dry washed and peeled boiled or raw broccoli florets, finely chop. You can also take frozen cabbage, just take it out of the freezer in advance and let it thaw in the refrigerator.

Wash the vegetables, cut off the ends from them, cut into small pieces. If the zucchini is young, do not peel off the peel, but if overripe, not only the skin but also the seeds must be removed. Wash the lettuce leaves, shake off the excess moisture, dry with a paper towel, and tear into pieces. Place all of the prepared ingredients in a blender and blend until smooth. If the drink seems very thick, dilute with yogurt and beat again.

Carrots & Spice Smoothie

Carrot juice is embellished in this recipe, which incorporates aromatic spices, sweet maple syrup, and creamy almond milk for one delicious smoothie that's packed with nutrition!

Ingredients

    2 cups carrots
    1 teaspoon ground ginger
    1 teaspoon cloves
    1 teaspoon cardamom
    1 teaspoon organic, natural maple syrup
    1 cup vanilla almond milk
    1/3 cup ice

How to Make

In a blender, combine the carrots, ginger, cloves, cardamom, maple syrup, and almond milk with ½ cup ice, and blend until thoroughly combined.

While blending, add the remaining ice until the desired consistency is achieved.

Pumpkin Smoothie with Apples

    Pumpkin is a tasty, healthy, low-calorie dietary product. Pumpkin pulp contains a lot of carotene, vitamins, and various minerals.

    This is a pumpkin apple smoothie recipe. This bright velvety drink will be enjoyed not only by adults but also children. For the preparation of this vitamin drink, both fresh and frozen pumpkin are suitable.

Ingredients

    1 cup pumpkin pulp (fresh or frozen)
    1 Apple
    1/2 cup Water
    2 tsp or to taste Honey
    0.5 tsp Cinnamon (optional)

Cut the pumpkin pulp into small pieces, steam until tender, then cool.

Cut the peeled apples into cubes.

Put the apple cubes and cooled pumpkin pieces into a blender glass, pour in the water, and puree.

Add the cinnamon. If you are not very fond of cinnamon, replace it with any other seasoning or eliminate it altogether.

For a sweeter smoothie, add honey or another sweetener to the drink. If the drink is thicker than you would like, add more water.

Whisk the contents of the glass again.

A bright and aromatic pumpkin smoothie with apples is ready. It is better to drink the drink immediately after preparation.

Pumpkin Citrus Smoothie with Ginger

There are many different pumpkin smoothie recipes. You can make a drink only from pumpkin, but the smoothie will turn out to be much tastier and healthier if you add berries, vegetables, or fruits to the pumpkin. This healthy, very gentle pumpkin smoothie with tart citrus notes will appeal to even the most sophisticated gourmet.

Ingredients

2 cups Pumpkin pulp (boiled)
1 Grapefruit
1 Orange
1-2 tbsp Honey - (to taste)
slice of ginger root
1/4 tsp Cinnamon - (to taste)
Nutmeg - a small pinch or to taste

How to Make

Peel the grapefruit and orange, divide into slices. Free the grapefruit pulp of the films. Place the citrus slices in a blender glass and beat on high speed. Pumpkin can be used raw in smoothies or you can steam the pumpkin and cool it. Cut the pumpkin pulp into small cubes or rub on a coarse grater. Add the cubes of pumpkin to a blender and beat until smooth. Add a sweetener - honey and aromatic spices: cinnamon, nutmeg, and ginger root grated on a fine grater. Beat the contents well. If you prefer a cool drink, add some ice cubes.

Pumpkin Pie

Who would have thought that pumpkin pie could actually be good for your health? This recipe combines the healthful ingredients of beta-carotene and fiber-rich pumpkin, along with a selection of original spices. You will love the delicious traditional pumpkin pie without any harmful additives.

Ingredients

   2 cups pure pumpkin puree
   1 teaspoon ground ginger
   1 teaspoon clove, ground
   1 teaspoon ground nutmeg and cinnamon
   1 cup vanilla almond milk
   1/4 glass of ice

How to Make

In a blender, combine pumpkin, ginger, cloves, nutmeg, cinnamon, and almond milk with ½ cup ice and beat until smooth. While stirring, add the remaining ice until the desired consistency is achieved.

Mint Cucumber

Despite being mostly water and fiber, cucumber is much more than just a delicious, moisturizing, and filling snack. Eating one serving of cucumbers a day will not only saturate your full serving of vegetables and satisfy your hunger, but also make sure your complexion stays - or becomes - clean and hydrated! And the mint in this smoothie will give you a refreshing coolness on a hot summer day.

Ingredients

2 peeled cucumbers
1 cup romaine lettuce
¼ cup chopped mint
1 cup of water
or 1/2 cup water
1/2 cup ice

How to Make

Rinse the lettuce and mint in running water, dry, remove coarse stems, if any. Cut the skin off the cucumber if it is too rough.

In a blender, combine the romaine lettuce, cucumber, mint, and ½ cup water and mix thoroughly.

Add the remaining water or ice (for cooling), stirring, until desired texture is achieved.

Green Health

A spicy, rich smoothie made with fresh vegetables and herbs - a modern alternative to the familiar salad. This vegetable slimming smoothie is also the healthiest.

Ingredients

1 cup young cabbage, chopped
1 cucumber
1/2 vegetable marrow
bunch of cilantro
1 cup pineapple chunks
1 glass of iced green tea
1/2 lemon juice
1 tbsp. l. grated ginger root
3-4 ice cubes

How to Make

Brew the green tea and refrigerate. Rinse the cilantro well and shake off the water. Chop the cabbage, cucumber, and zucchini. Grind all the ingredients for 1 minute on maximum blender power.

Add the green tea and lemon juice. Add a few ice cubes if desired to chill the smoothie. Stir again. Pour the drink into glasses and drink immediately.

Thick Tomato & Bell Pepper

The drink will appeal to fans of tomato juice and gazpacho.
This smoothie is best made from ground, well-ripened tomatoes.
Bell peppers should be fleshy and preferably red in color. Dill and rosemary add freshness to the drink, but it is worth adding them little by little so as not to spoil the main taste.

Ingredients

1 pc sweet bell pepper, preferably red
2 cups fresh meaty tomatoes
1/2 tablespoon olive or refined sunflower oil
dill and fresh rosemary
small lemon
mineral water (optional)

Cut the pepper lengthwise, remove the stalk, all the seeds, and soft partitions. After rinsing with water, cut the pulp into small pieces, pour them into a container for grinding.

Wash the tomatoes, rinse, and cut into slices. After removing the seals from the side of the stalk attachment, spread the tomatoes onto the pepper.

Add a small sprig of dill and some rosemary needles to the vegetables. Turn on the blender and work with it until you get a homogeneous mass.

Let the lemon stand in boiling water for two minutes. After cutting, squeeze the juice from the citrus. Filter it through a sieve, add 1/2 tablespoon to the smoothie.

Add the drink to taste, stir in the olive oil, shake well. Pouring into portions, immediately serve the tomato smoothie.

Sweet Pepper, Cucumber, & Ginger

I suggest you prepare a super healthy and body-cleansing drink from sweet green pepper, fresh cucumber, and ginger. Due to its composition, such a smoothie perfectly cleanses the intestines from the accumulated toxins and heavy metal salts. Try drinking a green smoothie every day, preferably at night, and your body will respond with gratitude, giving you vigor, energy, and a good mood.

Ingredients

½ green bell pepper
1 small fresh cucumber
a small piece of fresh ginger
1/2 cup green tea

How to Make

First, brew the green tea so that it has cooled down by the time you beat the ingredients.

Peel half of the sweet pepper from seeds and white partitions, cut into large pieces. Peel the cucumber and cut it into several pieces. Leave one cucumber ring to decorate the smoothie. Peel the root of the ginger and grate it on the shallow side of the grater.

Place pieces of bell pepper and cucumber in a blender, add the grated ginger and green tea. Whisk all of the ingredients for 1 minute at high speed.

Pour the finished green smoothie into a glass, garnish it with a cucumber ring and start smoothing. Bon Appetit!

Carrot Smoothie for a Great Mood

It is believed that orange is a great color to cheer you up and give positive emotions. Give a charge of positive energy in the morning, prepare a carrot smoothie from vegetables in a blender. Even children will like recipes with the addition of carrots and dried apricots.

Ingredients

5 small carrots
1 handful of dried apricots
0.5 lemon
0.5-1 glass of low-fat milk
1 tbsp. l. honey (to taste)

How to Make

Rinse the dried apricots under running water. Place in a bowl, cover with boiling water, leave for a few minutes.

Peel the carrots, cut them into pieces. Determine the size, depending on the power of your shredder. The lower it is, the smaller you make carrot slices for a vegetable smoothie. In the high-power blender, you can grind large and medium-sized pieces of hard vegetables.

Add the steamed dried apricots and milk to the bowl. Pour in half a glass first, then add more if needed. Grind until smooth. Add the liquid honey, stir and enjoy a nutritious drink.

Smoothie with Beetroot, Carrot, and Apple

A beetroot, apple, and carrot smoothie is a drink for proper nutrition or sports nutrition, and it will also be enjoyed by adherents of a raw food diet, as well as vegetarians. The drink has a detox effect, as well as a whole range of beneficial vitamins and minerals.

However, raw beets are not for everyone. It should be used with caution by people who have problems with the gastrointestinal tract, so if you wish, you can use baked or boiled beets.

Ingredients

Apple (green) - 2 pcs
Beets - 1 pc
Carrots - 1 pc
Honey - to taste
Water (drinking) - 1 glass

How to Make

Peel the carrots, apples, and beets, cut them into arbitrary pieces, and beat in a blender.

Add the honey and water and beat everything at high speed until smooth.

Cucumber Freshness

This smoothie will brighten up your hot day and quench your thirst. It is also great for dieters and will take its rightful place on the Lenten menu.

Ingredients

2 medium cucumbers
1 small green apple
a few stalks of celery
juice of half a lime
2-4 ice cubes
a pinch of salt and your favorite spices
a slice of ginger (optional)

How to Make

Core and peel the apple, cut the apple, cucumber, and celery into slices, and place in a blender bowl.

Add lime juice, salt, spices, and ice. If you want to get an original taste, grate a small piece of ginger. Stir all the ingredients until smooth.

You can add some ice cubes if you want a thinner smoothie.

Savory Zucchini with Herbs and Garlic

Garlic and pepper give the smoothie a spicy flavor, so it is easy to drink, despite its thick and rather coarse consistency. If you're not used to green smoothies, you can start with this option. This cocktail cleanses the intestines well and normalizes the water-salt balance. It is best consumed in the morning, an hour before breakfast, or instead of it.

Ingredients

  1 zucchini
  a small bunch of fresh parsley
  a small bunch of fresh dill
  a small bunch of spinach
  garlic - 1 clove;
  1 bell pepper (preferably green)
  1 cup yogurt or water

How to Make

Wash, dry, and chop the greens with a knife. Wash the zucchini, blot with a napkin and, without peeling, cut into small cubes. Cut the stalk off the pepper, extract the seeds from it. Cut the vegetable into small, free-form pieces.

Place all of the ingredients chopped with a knife into a jug of a blender, throw a clove of garlic in there, fill with kefir or filtered water. Turn on the blender and beat the food until smooth.

Beetroot & Strawberry Smoothie

A little pink for a bright start to the day! Beets are known for their powerful cleansing properties, while strawberries are rich in natural antioxidants. We are in a hurry to combine them into one drink.

Ingredients

4 beets
2 cups coconut or plain water
2 cups fresh or frozen strawberries
juice of 1 lime.

How to Make

Boil the skinless beets and mix with coconut or plain water.
Add fresh or frozen strawberries and 1 lime juice.
Stir in a blender until smooth.

Powerful Slimming Smoothie

Celery has a special place in a healthy diet, due to the nutrient content, which is why a drink based on it is very popular. In addition, celery contains a lot of fluid that flushes harmful substances out of the body.

Despite its harsh taste, celery goes well with many fruits and vegetables. All parts of this plant are edible, but the meatiest and juicy part is usually used for smoothies - the stems.

It is better not to drink this drink in the morning, since the digestive system has not yet begun to work at full strength, so it will be difficult for it to cope with celery and an apple. But, as a second breakfast or a healthy snack, such a drink is ideal.

Ingredients

2 stalks of celery
1 small bunch of parsley
1 kiwi
1 apple
1 tsp honey
1 cup mineral water without gas (you can use ordinary filtered water)
a few ice cubes (optional, for coolness)

How to Make

Wash the celery stalks, cut into small pieces, and place them in a blender bowl.

Rinse the parsley under running water, shake off the excess drops, chop finely so that large leaves do not get tangled in the blender knife, and immerse in a bowl with the celery.

Pour in some water, whisk, then pour in the rest of the water and run the blender again.

Wash the apple, cut it into slices, and place it in the bowl.

Peel the kiwi from the top layer, trim, and add to the rest of the smoothie.

Flavor your detox shake with honey or another sweetener if desired, blend everything with a blender until a smooth texture is obtained.

You can also add some ice cubes to keep the smoothie pleasantly cool.

Spicy Spinach

Not all people love greens, despite their beneficial properties. This smoothie is perfect for people like this because the spices in this smoothie mask the spinach flavor well.

The cinnamon in this smoothie gives an apple pie flavor, and the cloves make the flavor of this smoothie unique and unforgettable.

Ingredients

2 cups spinach
3 green apples, peeled and unpeeled
1 teaspoon cloves
1 teaspoon cinnamon
1½ cups coconut milk
a few ice cubes (optional)

How to Make

Rinse the spinach in running water and dry, place in a blender. Cut the apples into slices.

Add the spices to a blender and then the apples.

Slowly add coconut milk, stirring, until you get the desired consistency. If you want to cool the smoothie, add a few ice cubes and stir.

Pineapple-Ginger Smoothie with Spinach

This sugar-free Pineapple-Ginger Smoothie with Spinach is delicious, refreshing and best of all full of nutrients and vitamins! Try drinking a green smoothie every day, preferably at night, and your body will respond with gratitude, giving you vigor, energy, and a good mood.

Ingredients

½ cup Kale, stems discarded
1 cup Pineapple, frozen
½ Ginger Piece
1 cup Coconut Milk
1 tsp. Chia Seeds
1/3 cup Mint Leaves
½ cup Spinach Leaves
1 Lime, peel & rind removed

How to Make

To start, place all of the ingredients into a high-speed blender and blend for a minute or two or until you get a smooth drink. Serve immediately and enjoy.

Tip: If desired, you can add vegan protein powder to it.

Super Vitamin Bomb Smoothie

Everyone knows how healthy vegetables and greens are, but not everyone loves to eat them fresh, and even if they do, it is difficult to eat a large serving at a time. This super vegetable vitamin smoothie made from cucumber, kale, and spinach with orange juice solves this problem easily.

Ingredients

1 cup chopped cucumber
1 cup chopped kale or baby spinach
1/3 cup frozen mango
1 large sweet apple chopped
1 medium celery stalk, chopped (about 1/2 cup)
2 tablespoons hemp hearts
2 tablespoons fresh mint leaves
1 1/2 teaspoons virgin coconut oil (optional)
4-5 ice cubes
1/2 cup fresh red grapefruit or orange juice

How to Make

Wash the celery, spinach, and kale, dry, cut into small pieces, and place in the blender bowl. Wash the apple, cut it into wedges. The apple can be used with or without the peel.

Cut the skin off the cucumber if it is too rough. Add the rest of the smoothie ingredients to a high speed blender. Whisk for 1-2 minutes or until smooth and luxurious.

Next, transfer to a serving glass. Serve immediately and enjoy.

Spinach with Avocado and Grapes

This sweet green breakfast smoothie has it all: protein, fiber, vitamins, calcium, potassium, and other nutrients to energize you until lunchtime and even burn off excess fat.

Ingredients

15 pcs. Grapes green
1/2 Avocado
2 cups spinach leaves
1 Pear
1 cup natural yogurt
1-2 tablespoons Lime juice

How to Make

Wash the spinach leaves. Peel and cut the avocado, pear, green or red grapes into small pieces. Squeeze out the lime juice.
Whisk all of the ingredients in a blender.

Arugula & Avocado Detox Smoothie

I really love various greens and try to use them as often as possible: I add them to salads and green smoothies. This smoothie is probably one of my all-time favorite green cocktails. It has a very pleasant original taste, and a set of useful properties makes it perfect. Arugula plays a particularly important role in this detox smoothie.

Arugula has a pronounced mustard-peppery and slightly tart flavor, so I combined it with neutral flavor ingredients (apple and avocado) so as not to overpower the aroma of this healthy and tasty herb. I also added vitamin kiwi and lemon to balance the flavor.

Ingredients

100 g arugula
1/2 avocado
1 kiwi
1 apple
½ cup mineral water without gas (can be ordinary filtered)
1 tbsp. l. lemon or lime juice

For decoration
sunflower seeds
cranberry

Choose exclusively fresh arugula for smoothies. Rinse a bunch of arugula under running cold water and shake off the excess drops. Tear the leaves into smaller pieces so that the long stems do not interfere with whipping.

Peel the avocado from the top layer, remove the pit and cut into large pieces. Peel the kiwi and also cut it into large wedges. Remove the skin from the apple (you can leave it if you wish), cut the core out, and cut into pieces.

To make the drink as homogeneous as possible, first place the arugula in the blender bowl, then the fruit. Squeeze lime or lemon juice into the finished cocktail and stir for a couple of seconds. You do not need to add sweetener, so the taste of the drink will turn out to be more neutral with sourness.

Pour the smoothie into a glass, garnish with seeds and red berries such as cranberries.

Spinach & Apples Smoothies

As a very light-tasting green smoothie, the spinach and fruits in this recipe offer excellent amounts of nutrients from vitamin K to vitamin C to boost blood health and improve mood and balance. And if you want to slightly change the taste and increase the nutritional value, the water in this recipe can be replaced with any alternative milk.

Ingredients

2 cups spinach leaves
1 green apple, peeled and cored
2 ripe bananas, peeled
1 cup water

How to Make

Combine the spinach, bananas, apple, and ½ cup water in a blender, and blend thoroughly.

While blending, add the remaining water until the desired consistency is achieved.

Avocado & Spinach

For glowing skin, all you need to do is add ripe berries, healthy vegetables, juicy greens, and the right fats to your delicious smoothie recipe. Smoothies made from avocados, vegetables, and berries are a real vitamin "bomb" for the skin. Coconut milk is responsible for hydration, avocado for the right fats, and routine-rich blueberries and blueberries act as a firming cocktail.

Ingredients

1/2 avocado, peeled
1 rounded cup of spinach
1/2 cup frozen (or fresh) zucchini
1 banana
1 cup coconut milk (or other unsweetened plant-based milk)
1 tsp fresh ginger
a few ice cubes (optional)

How to Make

Freeze the zucchini. If you are using fresh zucchini, then add some ice cubes to the smoothie. Rinse the spinach in running water and dry.

Remove the pit from the avocado and cut it into pieces. Grate the ginger on a fine grater. Mix all the ingredients in a blender at high speed. Pour into a glass and sprinkle with your preferred treat.

Ginger Mint Smoothie

Delicious and very healthy mint and fruit smoothie recipe. This low-calorie, cleansing smoothie is a great addition to any diet.

The combination of mint, lemon, and ginger not only tones and cools, but also removes toxins from the body and restores metabolism.

Ingredients

1 kiwi
2 apples
1 cm ginger root (fresh)
4 sprigs of mint
2 leaves of lettuce or celery (optional)
2 tablespoons lime or lemon juice
1 tablespoons lemon zest
1 tablespoons honey
1/2 glass of still mineral water

Rinse the mint under running water and dry. Separate the mint leaves from the twigs. Pour the greens into a blender bowl, pour in the specified amount of mineral water, and beat until chopped.

Peel and core the apple and kiwi. Cut the fruit into slices and place it in the blender bowl with the herbs. Throw in a small portion of ginger root, previously peeled and chopped on a metal grater.

For a balanced flavor, add lemon juice and sweetener to the smoothie, and add some lemon zest for a more pronounced flavor. Whisk again with the fruit and toppings.

Pour the smoothie into tall glasses and enjoy!

Avocado, Kiwi & Parsley

An apple, avocado, and kiwi drink can be surprisingly well complemented with fresh parsley. With a very low calorie content (parsley is one of the ten most dietary products), it has the properties of restoring metabolism and cleansing the body.

Ingredients

1 avocado
1 kiwi
1 green apple
bunch of fresh parsley
1/2 glass of water
1/2 cup ice

How to Make

Rinse the parsley in running water and dry. Remove the pit from the avocado, peel the kiwi, peel the apple, cut everything into pieces, and put it in a blender. Add parsley and some of the water, stir. Then add water or ice in parts to obtain the desired consistency.

Super Vitamin Celery Smoothie

This combination of greens and juicy vegetables offers a healthy dose of fiber; vitamins A, C, and K; B vitamins; and various minerals, including iron and potassium, which, when combined, effectively fight water retention. But while this smoothie is healthy, the best part is that it's absolutely delicious!

Ingredients

1 cup spinach
3 stalks of celery
1 cucumber, peeled
1 carrot, peeled
1 glass of water

How to Make

Rinse the spinach and celery well in running water and shake off excess water. Cut the celery into slices. Peel the carrots and cut them into pieces with the cucumber.

Combine the spinach, celery, cucumber, carrots, and ½ cup water in a blender and beat until smooth.

Continue adding the remaining water as you blend until you get the texture you want.

Celery & Oatmeal

Such a vegetable smoothie with celery can completely replace breakfast since it contains complex carbohydrates and flax seeds that can satisfy the body for a long time.

Ingredients

2-3 Celery stalk
1 Cucumber
Spinach - a small bunch
Parsley - a small bunch
3 tablespoons Oatmeal
1 tablespoon Flaxseed
1 tablespoon Lemon juice
1 cup Cold Water
3-4 ice cubes (optional)

How to Make

Rinse the vegetables. Place the parsley and spinach in a blender. Cut the celery and cucumber and add to the herbs. Add the oatmeal and flax. It is advisable to grind the oatmeal in a coffee grinder before adding it.

Pour in the water (ice optional) and lemon juice, beat on high speed, pour into glasses, and serve.

Fruit & Berry Smoothies

Berry Vanilla Smoothie

This smoothie tastes rich, similar to berry yogurt, only healthier. This vitamin dessert is good to make to strengthen the immune system and maintain a great mood. Try it, you will like it!

Ingredients

1/2 cup Frozen Mixed Berries (blueberries, raspberries, strawberries, blueberries, etc.)
1 Banana, frozen
1 cup Vanilla Soy Milk
1/2 cup Almond milk
½ tsp. Mint Leaves

How to Make

Place all the ingredients needed to make the smoothie in a high-speed blender. Blend it for 2 to 3 minutes on a low speed or until smooth. Next, blend it again for another minute at a high speed. Finally, transfer to a serving glass and serve immediately.

Strawberries, Raspberries & Kiwi

This smoothie will delight the whole family - from kids to grandparents. In hot weather, it will come in handy: it can be served for an afternoon snack or even for lunch - it is an excellent substitute for heavy meals.

Ingredients

Strawberries, raspberries, blueberry - 1/3 cup each
1 banana
1 kiwi
1/2 cup coconut milk
1/2 cup apple juice
3-4 ice cubes
1 teaspoon of honey (optional)
mint and berries for decoration

How to Make

Wash the berries well. Peel the kiwi and banana and cut them into pieces and place them in a high-speed blender. Add coconut milk, ice, and apple juice. For a sweeter and thicker smoothie, add a teaspoon of honey. Blend it for 2 to 3 minutes on a low speed or until smooth. Next, blend it again for another minute at a high speed.

Tropical Fruit Spinach Smoothie

Tropical fruits along with spinach help to quickly improve digestion, while potassium-rich banana and coconut water (not to be confused with coconut milk) restore the body's water balance.

Ingredients

1/2 cup pineapple
1/2 cup papaya
1 banana
1 cucumber
1 cup coconut water
2 cups spinach
Ice a few cubes

How to Make

Cut the pineapple, papaya, banana, and cucumber into slices and place in the blender bowl. Whisk them in a blender with natural coconut water and spinach.

To cool the smoothie, add some ice and stir again. Pour the cocktail into glasses.

Raspberry Surprise

Delightful strawberry yogurt and coconut milk flavors are enhanced by the brilliant addition of raspberries to this delicious and nutritious smoothie. The rich red ingredients provide an antioxidant boost that will keep your body healthy and moving in the right direction!

Ingredients

2 cups raspberries
1 cup strawberry yogurt
1 cup coconut milk
¼ cup of ice

How to Make

In a blender, combine the raspberries, yogurt, and ½ cup coconut milk with ¼ cup ice and beat until smooth.

While stirring, add the remaining coconut milk and ice until the desired consistency is achieved.

Vanilla Mango Smoothie

Ingredients

1 Mango (about 1 cup chopped)
1 Banana, frozen
1 cup Vanilla Soy Milk
1 cup Ice Cubes
⅛ cup unsweetened coconut
1 teaspoon vanilla
1 tablespoon Maple Syrup
1 tbsp. Chia Seeds

How to Make

To start with, place all of the ingredients needed to make the smoothie in a high-speed blender.Blend it for 2 to 3 minutes on a low speed or until smooth. Next, blend it again for another minute at a high speed or until frothy. Finally, transfer to a serving glass and serve immediately.

Pineapple Perfection

Coconut meat, banana, and pineapple give this delicious smoothie its unique flavor and texture. But this combination provides more than just beauty and taste; Vitamin C and phytochemicals like bromelain boost immunity, improve system function, and make this smoothie a versatile winner!

Ingredients

½ cup pineapple
1 banana, peeled
1 cup coconut meat
2 cups coconut milk
½ glass of ice

How to Make

In a blender, combine the coconut, banana, pineapple, and coconut milk with ½ cup ice and beat until smooth. While stirring, add the remaining ice until the desired consistency is achieved.

Spicy Ginger-Pear Surprise

The sweet and unique flavor of delicious pears paired with an aromatic blend of spicy ginger, cloves, and cardamom creates an even more sensual sensation in a nutritious smoothie. And if that wasn't enough, this smoothie is also filled to the brim with plenty of magnesium, which acts as fuel to ignite your metabolic fire!

Ingredients

2 uncored pears
1 teaspoon ground ginger
1 teaspoon ground cloves
1 teaspoon ground cardamom
2 glasses of water
1 glass of ice

How to Make

In a blender, combine the pears, ginger, cloves, cardamom, and 1 cup water with ½ cup ice and beat until smooth. While stirring, add the remaining water and ice until the desired consistency is achieved.

Lemon Banana Smoothie

In the heat, you always want something cool and refreshing. And what could be better than a delicious vitamin smoothie? Probably just a light lemon-banana drink with nut milk.

Lemons help cleanse the body and restore the acid-base balance. Almond milk gives the drink a delicate creamy taste, making the smoothie even tastier and more aromatic. This recipe will also help normalize cholesterol levels and improve digestion.

If you don't have almond milk on hand, you can substitute it with any other nut, soy, or natural yogurt.

Ingredients

1 1/2 almond milk
1/2 lemon
1 banana
1 vanilla pod
1 tbsp. l. honey
ice cubes
mint leaves for decoration

How to Make

Peel the banana, cut it into slices, or divide it into several pieces and place them in the blender bowl. Cut the lemon into two halves. Remove the zest from one part of the lemon and squeeze the juice. Pour the lemon juice into the banana bowl.

Add almond milk to a bowl. Add honey for sweetness and half the vanilla seeds for flavor.

Whisk all of the smoothie ingredients at maximum speed until smooth and tender.

Pour the smoothie into glasses or smoothie glasses. Add ice. Add straws to the drink and garnish each serving with lemon zest and a sprig of lemon balm or mint.

Peach Surprise

Filled with peaches and nectarines, this smoothie is packed with powerful antioxidants like beta-carotene, and tastes amazing at the same time! This combination of ingredients will pleasantly surprise you and give you an unforgettable taste!

Ingredients

1 cup pitted peaches
1 cup pitted nectarines
1 banana, peeled
1 cup of white tea, chilled
½ cup of ice

How to Make

In a blender, combine peaches, nectarines, banana, and white tea with ½ cup ice and beat until smooth.

While stirring, add the remaining ice until the desired consistency is achieved.

Banana Strawberry Chia Smoothie

Ingredients

1/3 cup frozen mango
1 cup frozen strawberries
1 large ripe banana
2 cup Vanilla Soy Milk
1 tablespoon chia seeds
1 tablespoon wheat germ (optional)

How to Make

In a blender, combine the coconut, banana, pineapple, and coconut milk with ½ cup ice and beat until smooth.

While stirring, add the remaining ice until the desired consistency is achieved.

Spicy Cherry Smoothie

Creamy, spicy, and sweet, this smoothie is a great way to add some nutritious fruit servings to it. The vitamin C in dark red berries helps protect against heart disease and prenatal problems. This delicious recipe takes your healthy lifestyle to the next level!

Ingredients

2 cups pitted cherries
1 tablespoon grated ginger
1 teaspoon ground cloves
1 teaspoon ground nutmeg
1 cup vanilla almond milk
½ glass of ice
½ glass of water

How to Make

In a blender, combine the cherries, ginger, cloves, nutmeg, and almond milk with ½ cup ice, and blend until thoroughly combined.

While blending, add the water and remaining ice until the desired consistency is achieved.

Cherries & Banana

If you're like most people, banana splits bring back memories of carefree childhood bliss. Here, instead of using processed ice cream and additives, this smoothie uses all-natural ingredients that are packed full of B vitamins and vitamin C.

Ingredients

¼ cup cherries, pitted
2 bananas, peeled
½ cup coconut meat
1 cup plain yogurt
½ cup water
½ cup ice

How to Make

In a blender, combine the bananas, coconut meat, cherries, plain yogurt, and ½ cup water with ½ cup ice, and blend until thoroughly combined.

While blending, add the remaining water and ice until the desired consistency is achieved.

Blueberry Pineapple Smoothie

This shake features blueberries, kale, pineapple, and unsweetened yogurt, plus highly nutritious and healthy avocados. Nutritionists say the combination of these products is ideal for making a fat-burning smoothie.

Blueberries and almond oil are included in this cocktail for a reason – they have been proven to be one of the few foods that help burn belly fat (naturally, coupled with physical activity).

Ingredients

1/2 cup Blueberries
1/2 cup Pineapple
1 cup Kale
1/2 cup natural yogurt
1 tbsp Almond oil
3/4 cup Water

How to Make

Chop the kale and cut the pineapple into slices. Place them in a blender bowl and stir. Add the berries, almond oil, and yogurt and stir again.

Add the water gradually to the consistency you need. You can also add a couple of ice cubes for coolness. Whisk all of the ingredients until smooth.

Summer Apple Banana Smoothie

This simple and sweet smoothie combines the familiar and favorite flavors of apples and bananas and turns them into a cool, icy treat.

The addition of pure apple juice gives this already sweet blend an apple flavor that helps blend everything together for the perfect flavor!

Ingredients

1 banana, peeled
1 yellow apple with a core
1 cup of natural, organic apple juice (not from concentrate)
1/3 glass of ice

How to Make

In a blender, combine the banana, apple, and apple juice with ½ cup ice and beat until smooth.

While stirring, add the remaining ice until the desired consistency is achieved.

Apple & Pineapple

Who would've thought that the sweet (but tart!) flavors of pineapple could go so well with the light taste of an apple? Simple, sweet, and whipped up in just minutes, this smoothie provides a delicious treat any time of day.

Ingredients

2 cups pineapple
1 red apple, cored
1 cup organic, pure apple juice (not from concentrate)
½ cup ice

How to Make

In a blender, combine the pineapple, apple, and apple juice with ½ cup ice, and blend until thoroughly combined.

While blending, add the remaining ice until the desired consistency is achieved.

Cream Peaches

This smoothie combines rich, aromatic, natural ingredients that give Peaches 'n' Cream its amazing taste.

It's hard to resist such a temptation!

Ingredients

2 cups pitted peaches
1 cup yogurt
½ cup of water
½ cup of ice

How to Make

In a blender, combine the peaches, kefir, and water with ½ cup ice and beat until smooth.

While stirring, add the remaining ice until the desired consistency is achieved.

Spicy Ginger-Strawberry Smoothie

The piquancy of this smoothie comes from the addition of delicious ginger, which makes every sip a memorable one! Contains antioxidants for immunity, protein for strength and endurance, and probiotics for good protection against bacteria. The combination of ingredients in this recipe helps make life so much tastier!

Ingredients

2 cups strawberries
1 tablespoon grated ginger
1 glass of natural yogurt
1 glass of ice

How to Make

In a blender, combine the strawberries, ginger, and yogurt with ½ cup ice and beat until smooth. While mixing, add the remaining ice until the desired consistency is achieved.

Iced Apple & Spice Smoothie

This frosty smoothie, which is packed with apples and delicious spices, will likely make you think of a delicious apple pie.

Ingredients

2 yellow apples, cored
1 teaspoon ground cinnamon
1 teaspoon ground cloves
1 teaspoon ground ginger
1 cup all-natural, organic apple juice (not from concentrate)
1/4 cup ice

How to Make

In a blender, combine the apples, cinnamon, cloves, ginger, and apple juice with ½ cup ice, and blend until thoroughly combined.

While blending, add the remaining ice until the desired consistency is achieved.

Gooseberry & Blackberry Mint Smoothie

On a hot summer day, you want to drink something refreshing. Peppermint is the perfect ingredient for any tonic or smoothie. I decided to add a touch of gooseberry and blackberry to this mint smoothie. If you want to sweeten this smoothie, use honey or other natural sweeteners.

Ingredients

1 handful of blackberries
1 handful of gooseberries
1 banana
2-3 sprigs of fresh peppermint
1 ½ tbsp. natural yogurt
1 tsp poppy (optional)

For decoration (optional):
Fresh mint - 4 leaves
Poppy - 1 pinch
Blackberry

Rinse the mint sprigs in cold water, then separate the leaves from the stems. Sort the gooseberries carefully, remove the green tails. Rinse the berries well with a sieve. Sort the blackberries thoroughly and wash them as well.

Put mint leaves in a blender, add gooseberries and blackberries, and add poppy seeds. Fill all the ingredients with yogurt.

Run the blender at full power and beat until smooth. Pour the finished mint smoothie into portioned glasses. Garnish with berries, mint leaves, or a pinch of poppy seeds.

Wonderful Watermelon Smoothie

This delicious smoothie is packed full of hydrating watermelon, smooth banana, and creamy coconut milk that will brighten your day. With flu-fighting quercetin and cancer-fighting lycopene brimming in every sip of this simple splendor, your vitality can improve without any effort at all!

Ingredients

2 cups watermelon
1 banana, peeled
1 cup coconut milk
1 cup ice

How to Make

In a blender, combine the watermelon, banana, and coconut milk with ½ cup ice, and blend until thoroughly combined.

While blending, add the remaining ice until the desired consistency is achieved.

Crazy Savory Cranberries Smoothie

Cranberries lend a tart sweetness to any smoothie, and when paired with delicious ginger, there's no end to the amazing depth of flavors.

Helping to maintain urinary tract health, the cranberries' powerful benefits make this smoothie a great option for everyone of every age and gender.

Ingredients

2 cups cranberries
1 tablespoon grated ginger
1 cup vanilla rice milk
1 cup ice

How to Make

In a blender, combine the cranberries, ginger, and rice milk with ½ cup ice, and blend until thoroughly combined.

Smoothie Desserts

Strawberry with Ice Cream and Pistachios

This delicate strawberry smoothie with ice cream and pistachios is a super tasty vitamin drink and perfectly refreshes you in the heat. Strawberries contain a record amount of nutrients and are the main source of minerals. The antioxidants contained in strawberries make the skin supple and firm, and folic acid is essential for the normal functioning of the reproductive system.

Ingredients

2 cups fresh or frozen strawberries
200 g ice cream
2 tablespoon peeled pistachios
a few ice cubes (optional)

How to Make

Wash the strawberries, sort them out, remove the sepals. Cut large berries into several parts. Pour the ripe berries into the chopper bowl. Let's add a delicious high-quality ice cream. Pour the peeled pistachios into the mixture.

Whisk the ingredients in a high-speed blender for a minute to make the smoothie tender and smooth. You can add some ice cubes to keep the smoothie cool.

Pour the drink into transparent glasses or wine glasses, decorate each portion with strawberries and a straw. Serve immediately.

Smoothie Tropical Paradise

Tropical Paradise is the phrase that best describes the aroma and flavor of this deliciously sweet smoothie, which combines the aromas of coconut, banana, vanilla, aromatic spices, sweet maple syrup, and almonds. A combination of nutrients like B vitamins and rich minerals found in every sip will help protect your blood, brain, and heart from harm.

Ingredients

1 cup coconut meat
1 banana, peeled
1 vanilla pulp
1 teaspoon ground cloves
1 teaspoon ground ginger
1 teaspoon natural organic maple syrup
2 cups vanilla almond milk
1 cups ice

How to Make

In a blender, combine the coconut, banana, vanilla bean pulp, cloves, ginger, maple syrup, and almond milk with 1/2 cup ice and stir until combined.While mixing, add the remaining ice until the desired consistency is achieved.

Chocolate Cherry Smoothie

This smoothie turns out to be tasty, healthy, and rich. And all thanks to the classic combination of cherries and cocoa, complemented by almond milk. The endorphins produced by the body under the influence of cocoa always result in a good mood.

This recipe uses frozen cherries, but you can use fresh cherries, but then you will need to add a frozen banana or half a cup of ice cubes to keep them cool. Almond milk can be substituted with any plant milk or water.

Ingredients

2 cups frozen cherries
1 cup almond milk / any other plant-based milk/water
2 tablespoons raw cocoa powder
1 small pitted royal date, chopped (optional)
2 tablespoons of almond paste (urbech) (optional)

For decoration:
raw cocoa beans
hemp

How to Make

If using fresh cherries, add 0.5 cups of ice cubes or 1 frozen banana and reduce the amount of cherries to 1.5 cups. First, pour in only 0.5 cups of milk, adding the rest as needed.

Place all of the ingredients in a blender and blend until smooth, add some more milk if necessary.

Serve garnished with toppings of your choice. Eat with a spoon.

Strawberry Banana Smoothie Dessert

Sometimes you want to pamper yourself with a tasty, but not very high-calorie dessert. I prepared the drink from the most affordable products - banana and frozen strawberries. The cream gives the fruit smoothie a nice creamy taste and it felt like I was eating delicious ice cream when tasting the drink. Only whipped cream has a clear advantage over ice cream – it is light and airy, so you will need very little of it.

Ingredients

1 banana
1/2 cup strawberries
1-2 tablespoons whipped cream 20% fat
a pinch of ground cinnamon
1 tsp fresh honey
1/4 cup berry juice

Remove the frozen strawberries from the freezer and leave the berries to defrost for 5 minutes in a warm place.

Peel the banana and cut it into slices.

Throw the strawberries and banana slices into the blender bowl, add berry juice and honey.

Whisk the dessert ingredients for 1 minute on medium speed.

Pour the smoothie into a clear glass.

Shake the can of cream well and, turning it upside down, squeeze a pile of cream (about 5 cm in height) onto the surface of the smoothie.

Sprinkle the drink with a pinch of cinnamon and garnish with berries or a banana ring.

Serve the strawberry-banana dessert with cream on the table.

Bon Appetit!

Banana-Pistachio Smoothie with Cocoa

This drink has an interesting taste, so all the members of your family will definitely like it. I deliberately added quite a bit of chocolate to the drink, but when you taste this dessert, you will think that there is more than enough of it.

If you and your kids have a sweet tooth, then this smoothie will be an excellent alternative to fatty and high-calorie cakes and pastries. It is for this reason that I love smoothie desserts so much: they are very sweet and tasty, but low in calories.

Ingredients

2 banana
1 tsp cocoa powder
1 cup natural yogurt
2 tsp peeled and chopped pistachios
2 tsp grated milk chocolate

Peel the banana and cut it into several pieces. Put the chocolate in the freezer for a few minutes, so that later it can be easily grated. Remove the shells from the nuts and rub them a little between your palms, removing the excess husk.

Throw the pistachios into the blender bowl first and chop them at high speed. Next, add the banana pieces, yogurt, and cocoa to the pistachio chips. Whisk all of the ingredients for 1 minute.

Pour the finished smoothie into a glass. Remove a piece of chocolate from the freezer and rub it on the shallow side of the grater directly over the drink. Insert a straw into the smoothie and serve. Bon Appetit!

Banana, Kiwi, and Creamy Ice Cream Smoothie

I have ice cream in my freezer. I decided that just eating ice cream is boring, we'd better make a delicious smoothie out of it. This smoothie is loved by both children and adults.

Very few ingredients are required: ripe fruit, some honey, and ground cinnamon for flavor. A few minutes - and now we have a ready-made healthy drink that will energize you for the whole day.

Ingredients

2 bananas
3 kiwi
1 pack of ice cream
2 tsp honey
0.5 tsp ground cinnamon

Peel the bananas and kiwis that have been pre-cooled in the refrigerator. Let's cut them into mugs. We will leave a few slices to decorate the finished smoothie.

Add the chopped fruits to the blender bowl, then add the ice cream. For flavor, add ground cinnamon. If you like sugary drinks, add a little sugar, or even better, liquid honey - this will be healthier.

Beat the smoothie until smooth. Now it remains to grind everything at high speed so that the fruit turns into a puree and combines well with the ice cream.

Gently pour the drink into bowls or wide glasses. Decorate the smoothie with a slice of kiwi and sprinkle with cinnamon. That's all, now you can enjoy a delicious and healthy smoothie with ice cream and fruit.

Banana Almond Chocolate Smoothie

Breakfast is the most important meal of the day, energizing you for the whole day. Having a hearty breakfast fills the body with all the necessary elements at the very moment when it needs it the most.

To make my drink more satisfying and replace breakfast, I add almond milk, bananas, oatmeal, natural chocolate to it. And if you combine all these components, you get a mega nutritious cocktail that guarantees high performance throughout the day, as well as clarity of mind and excellent mood.

Ingredients

1 banana;
1 glass of almond milk
1 tablespoon of almond oil
2 tablespoon oatmeal;
2 tablespoon natural dark chocolate;

a pinch of cinnamon or nutmeg;
For decoration
coconut flakes, sesame seeds, almonds, banana slices, chocolate chips.

How to Make

Pour about half the almond milk into the blender bowl. Add the banana, previously peeled, and cut it into random pieces. Also, before using the banana, it is better to freeze it a little in the freezer compartment, this will give the drink a creamy texture, and also cool it significantly.

Add the dark chocolate chunks, almond butter, and banana chunks, and stir in the oatmeal. Whisk the contents of the blender until a homogeneous mass is formed.

Then add the rest of the milk, season with a pinch of cinnamon or nutmeg, and whisk the mixture again.

Pour the smoothie into a serving bowl and add the toppings suggested in the ingredients list.

Bon Appetit!

Apricot-Coffee & Chocolate Smoothie

I think you will appreciate my thick chocolate-coffee cocktail with dried apricots, which combines bitter-spicy and sweet tastes, and you will also remember the unusual aftertaste with a divine aroma for a long time. Chocolate is a source of energy. The most useful is dark chocolate - it contains a lot of magnesium and potassium. Caffeine promotes the mental activity of the brain, improves mood, prevents drowsiness, tones, and adds strength and energy.

You do not need to consume this smoothie after meals, this dessert can be considered a complete meal.

Ingredients

1/4 cup of natural coffee
3-4 pieces of dried apricots
1 banana
2 tablespoon grated dark chocolate
1/3 cup coconut milk
1 tablespoon chopped walnuts
a pinch of cinnamon or vanilla
a pinch of nutmeg
chocolate balls (dry breakfast) for decoration

How to Make

Brew the coffee however works best for you, set it aside so that it cools completely. Then strain with a metal sieve, completely separating the liquid from the sediment. Pour the coffee liquid into the blender container.

Peel the banana and cut it into slices, put in the freezer for 30 minutes.

Rinse the dried apricots and soak them in water for a while to soften them, then cut them into small pieces.

Place all of the prepared ingredients in a blender, sprinkle with cinnamon and nutmeg, beat the mixture until smooth.

Then add the coconut milk until the consistency you want is formed and beat again.

Chocolate Black Bean Smoothie

Ingredients

1 Banana, frozen
½ cup Black Beans
3-4 large dates
1 tsp. Cinnamon, ground
1 cup Cauliflower, frozen
1 tbsp. Hemp Seeds
1 tbsp. Cocoa Powder
1 cup Almond Milk

How to Make

Start by placing all of the ingredients needed to make the smoothie in a high-speed blender.

Blend them for 1 to 2 minutes or until smooth and luxurious.

Next, transfer to a serving glass

Serve immediately and enjoy.

Tip: For the topping, you can use cacao nibs.

Conclusion

Smoothies are top of the simplest, healthiest, and fastest diets anyone could have.

They are relatively convenient to make, and you can supplement some deficiencies in your nutrients through them.

With smoothies, you can detoxify, fight germs and infections, and up your weight loss game.

When making a smoothie, you do not simply pick the fruits and randomly dump them in a blender. There are several factors to consider. There are tips to learn too.

These and several others lessons must be clear to you before you attempt to make smoothies. There are ways to sweeten your smoothie without side effects. There are several types and categories too.

This complex world may not be clear to you as a newbie or someone who's never paid serious attention to smoothies' dietary information. Not to worry, I have taken enough time to provide a bit-by-bit explanation of them in this book. No doubt, you are going to move from a complete beginner to someone who understands the art of smoothies.

I truly hoped you learned a great deal.
Cheers!

Made in the USA
Las Vegas, NV
15 July 2022